THE MACHINERY OF FINANCE
AND THE
MANAGEMENT OF STERLING

The Machinery of Finance and the Management of Sterling

A. T. K. Grant

C.B., C.M.G.
Fellow of Pembroke College, Cambridge

MACMILLAN · London · Melbourne · Toronto
ST MARTIN'S PRESS · New York
1967

SOCIAL
SCIENCES

Lipman fund

© A. T. K. Grant 1967

Published by
MACMILLAN & CO LTD
4 Little Essex Street London WC2
and also at Bombay Calcutta and Madras
Macmillan South Africa (Publishers) Pty Ltd Johannesburg
The Macmillan Company Australia Pty Ltd Melbourne
The Macmillan Company of Canada Ltd Toronto
St Martin's Press Inc New York

Library of Congress Catalog Card no. 68–10532

Printed in Great Britain by
WESTERN PRINTING SERVICES LIMITED, BRISTOL

Contents

		page
	Preface	7
1	Introduction	11
2	Payment and Liquidity	
	1. The Structure of Obligations	20
	2. The Settlement of Obligations	22
	3. Assets and Liabilities	25
	4. Liquidity and Insolvency	29
	5. Liquidity and the Concept of Money	31
	6. The Return on Assets and the Concept of Interest	35
	7. Implications of Liquidity	37
3	Banks and Intermediaries as Borrowers	
	1. The System in Outline	41
	2. The Allocation of Personal Savings	46
	3. The Temporary Investment of Business Funds	56
	4. The Banks and their Depositors	61
4	Banks and Intermediaries as Lenders	
	1. Banks and their Assets	68
	2. The Cumulative Creation of Credit	73
	3. The Banks, the Bank of England and the Discount Market	78
	4. Liquidity and the Indebtedness of the Public Sector	84
	5. Other Banks and Financial Institutions	90
5	The Mechanics of Control	
	1. The Scope of Financial Control	95

2. General Quantitative Credit Controls   97
3. Discriminatory Credit Controls   107
4. Control and Money Rates   109
5. Some Implications of Control   114

6   The External Position of Sterling
1. The Components of the External Balance   121
2. Sterling Between the Wars: The Convertible Floating Pound   125
3. Sterling After 1945: Fixed Exchanges and Convertibility for Non-Residents   128
4. The International Market in Expatriate Currencies   132
5. Methods and Objectives in the International Management of Sterling   147
6. International Acceptance Business as against International Deposit Banking   154

7   Financial Reform
1. The Economic Deadlock   160
2. The Structure of Short-Term Finance   162
3. The Provision of Longer-Term Capital   172
4. Sterling and International Payments   179
5. Some Further Implications of Liquidity   183

Index   187

Preface

This book is concerned with our financial arrangements and institutions, with their bearing both on economic progress at home and on the strength of the pound abroad, and with the way in which they are being operated in face of developments which are pressing upon us.

We have recognised the need to maintain a high and stable level of employment, and have accepted the economic consequences that go with it. We must be prepared to see some tendency for prices to go on rising. We become concerned with matters which include: the future of fixed-interest lending, whether by Government, business undertakings or individuals; the balance between fixed-interest and participating investment; the taxation of fixed-interest income when eroded by rising values. There are institutional implications: methods of financial control in an economy run under pressure; the devolution of responsibility for decision-making when matters can no longer be left to settle themselves; the implications of new money markets and differential rates of interest.

There are corresponding matters in the overseas field: the international liquidity problem, including that of the price of gold and of gold-hoarding, and the future of the reserve currencies. For the U.K. in particular there is a double problem on international account. Not only is there the deficit on the current balance of payments (of which we are all aware), but also the situation when the growth of short-term liabilities balanced by long-term assets gives rise to a liquidity difficulty over and above that coming from a deficit on current account, a difficulty which persists even when the deficit is dealt with.

In interpreting these phenomena I have made use of a general concept of liquidity related to that of the Radcliffe Report. This liquidity arises out of the composition and distribution of assets and liabilities—present and prospective—of every spending person or agency, and defines the extent to which the spender can meet his obligations, and accordingly the scale on which he can safely enter into fresh commitments. Obligations are settled by offsetting assets and liabilities; the process is operated (mainly, though not entirely) through the banking system. The controlling mechanism is that of the rules governing access to this machinery of cancellation. Such an approach can I hope throw new light on the present position and point to ways in which some of the problems might constructively be handled.

We are dealing with technical matters which have very considerable consequences. What I have to say will I hope be of interest to those with a general or specialised experience of finance; to economists who are not preoccupied with other aspects of their work; to students of finance; perhaps also to the general reader who is prepared for some moderately hard going because of a compelling interest in current economic affairs. With this wide range of interests in mind, I have on the one hand tried—in order not to break the thread—to restrict extraneous matter to background material which helps to make clear the argument, and on the other hand retained some pieces of repetition and rather simple exposition in an attempt to ease the path of those to whom part of the ground may be unfamiliar.

It remains for me to acknowledge my debts. Cambridge has provided me with an environment and an opportunity for developing ideas with which I began to wrestle when I wrote about the British capital market more years ago than I care to remember, and which then remained in a state of gnawing suspension during a long interval of Government service. In developing these ideas I have been influenced by the writings of

Professor Richard Sayers and aided by the information made available in the illuminating *Quarterly Bulletin* published by the Bank of England. I have learned much from talk—east of Fleet Street, west of Aldgate—with those who have generously given time to explain the workings of their business. I owe a debt to Michael Posner and to an unidentified reader from Macmillans for the stern but sympathetic care with which they went through the draft of this book, much to its benefit; the defects which remain are mine. Finally, I am indebted to my wife Helen for her tolerance of a neglectful husband, for the book was written under pressure at a time when there were many things to do.

Pembroke College, Cambridge
June 1967   A. T. K. G.

CHAPTER ONE

Introduction

The subject-matter of this book is the machinery of finance and its effective operation. The machinery is that of the United Kingdom in the second half of the 1960s. In covering the ground one may also hope to discover experiences of relevance elsewhere.

Machinery here means: banks, intermediaries and associated financial enterprises, together with those institutions of government concerned with financing the public sector and with the monetary management of the economy.

The purpose of this study is to examine the organisation of finance and its working in contemporary conditions. This requires an account of the main features of the system sufficient to show what it does and why in certain circumstances it behaves as it does. We need in particular to see how it has reacted and is likely to react to the strains with which it is faced and the demands made upon it, and what is the scope for introducing deliberate improvements.

One must begin by asking: what do we expect from the financial machine? On the positive side: that it should meet effectively and fairly the reasonable requirements of the private individual, of the business community and of the public authorities. On the negative side: that it should avoid being a source of instability. This much is common ground. In addition the machine should be a flexible instrument for the implementation of economic policy, sensitive to handling and smooth and responsive in operation. This too is now widely accepted, though acceptance took time in coming.

This last requirement is in part an outcome of the Keynesian revolution in economic thinking. *The General Theory*[1] put the maintenance and control of effective demand in the centre of the economic scene where it displaced doctrines which looked to the free working of a competitive price system as carrying its own remedies. The case as put by Keynes, together with the contrasting experience of inter-war unemployment and the full employment of the post-war years, started a transformation in men's views on such matters.

In present circumstances our concern is not with unemployment and deficiency of demand, but with the full employment of resources and its associated problems. Those in charge of finance are left with deliberate decisions which require to be implemented, and the need of a machine which can make those decisions effective. Much in the following pages will be concerned with what follows from this, for even if the main force in maintaining or controlling demand must be sought in the sphere of taxation and public expenditure, the financial machine is always involved in making this policy effective, and in particular is concerned with matters of technical detail which can have significant consequences.

The central themes of the contemporary approach are thus the full employment of resources and the maintenance and control of demand. By implication, the objective is that the level of demand should be so managed as to ensure that the pressure on resources is adequate to secure their effective utilisation without becoming excessive. In an industrialised country such as Britain excessive pressure will first show itself in the labour market rather than in a shortage of productive facilities.

The reason is this. Once we assume that all the labour required is available, successive additions to output can be made over much of the field at a cost which is increasing, but not very sharply. Obsolescent machinery can be kept in being

---

[1] J. M. Keynes, *The General Theory of Employment, Interest and Money* (Macmillan, 1936). It is well to recall when this appeared, midway between the Great Depression and the Second World War.

alongside the replacements that are coming in. Existing plant can be worked—even overworked—by being used more intensively. Greater wear and tear and more night shifts cost money, but not all that money. And production facilities can be added to after an interval, if necessary with the help of equipment imported from outside. Given the required manpower, it is possible to meet an appreciable increase in demand from existing productive facilities without incurring an intolerable burden, while the scale of these facilities can be increased given a moderate lapse of time.

With full employment things are otherwise. Everything is different if the manpower is not there. One is up against what is very nearly an absolute limit. More workers are not available. There is a point beyond which people are not prepared to work more hours in the week, however generous the overtime pay and extra bonuses. If the pressure of demand continues, there will be a scramble for labour, wages will start sailing up as employers bid against each other, while output may remain unchanged. Labour becomes—spectacularly—the limiting factor. (One should perhaps add that the position will be otherwise in a developing country, where there are likely to be large reserves of labour available, though even here a shortage of skilled labour could produce not dissimilar results.)

All this comes back to the flow of effective demand. Between the wars the economy suffered from a deficiency. If effective demand is at too low a level, the rates of return available from acquiring existing income-producing assets at current market levels will in general be relatively more favourable than the prospective returns offered in respect of the creation of new assets, and the demand for them will fall to lower levels. This in its turn will have a cumulative effect which (in the absence of countervailing action) will show itself in the appearance of unemployed or under-employed resources, human and material. Conversely, an increase in demand will both increase the value of current assets and improve the prospective returns from new productive expansion; the increase will become cumulative; and if this is allowed to continue, one may get to the point where the barrier of manpower shortage imposes a limit on output. Once that is reached, further increases in demand are reflected in higher costs, in particular in increased wage bills, and in growing imports and falling exports.

For reasons such as these, the concept of a flow of demand managed in the general interest has come to play so important a part in economic policy-making. The role of finance in this process is in a sense subsidiary: once one accepts that the financial machine cannot by itself provide the answer, and that considered decisions on policy are required, such decisions have to be taken elsewhere. But the part of finance in the implementation of these decisions can nevertheless be critical. Decision-making postulates the existence of machinery capable of bringing decisions into effect. Available facilities, and access to them, the nature of the standards applied, the costs and charges involved, can all help or hinder the translation of the major decisions into detailed commitments. The work of the bank manager becomes harder when he has to consider not only the capacity of his customer to repay, but also whether what his customer really wants to do fits in with some overall requirement imposed in the general interest. Rules of thumb become more elaborate, distinctions requiring discriminating judgement are more frequent, and broad overall concepts call for more and more technical elaborations.

In this setting the inherited ideas appropriate to a semi-autonomous monetary system lose relevance. These took as their starting-point the concept of something objective—money —which had an existence of its own independent of the transactions for which it might be used. This money was something which could be measured; that is, its total could be calculated. The volume of payments which it could be called on to sustain was ultimately geared to the amount of money in existence. A shortage or excess of money could be reflected in the charge made for it—the rate of interest. Behind the various refinements, there was always money which could be counted, and a rate of interest which was expected to move in response to supply and demand.

Not only have such basic assumptions become by now dangerously irrelevant, but even the associations of such words as 'money' and 'interest' can in themselves mislead. The traditional descriptions of the functions of money—unit of account, medium of exchange, store of value—date from an age when gold coins were in circulation. No normal person builds up stores of bank-notes; it is safer and less unprofitable to turn them in to some institution which pays interest on deposits. No one uses notes and coin except as counters convenient for settling the smaller transactions; in paying by cheque we are not using money as a medium of exchange, but rather as a convenient measure in the course of a larger accounting process. Even the concept of money as a unit of account calls for caution, at a time when for comparison over time values and assessments recorded in monetary units have to be noted in some such way as 'at 1958 prices'.

There is a further danger in uses of the word 'money' which imply that it can conveniently be quantified. The Quantity of Money (in a country where many of us make payments by drawing on overdrafts) or additions to the Money Supply (while leaving doubts as to what is being added to what) are concepts so tinged with deceptive associations that it is wise (one would suggest) to avoid them wherever they are the foundation on which a closely argued proposition is to be erected. Less coloured words like 'finance' or 'means of payment' are free of such associations, and have the merit that they force us to make clear what we mean.

It is prudent to beware even of such a concept as *the* rate of interest. In the economic literature of the earlier twentieth century a sort of Platonic synthesis of all rates of interest appears in various guises. If there were no departure from this ideal rate of interest (sometimes described as 'real', sometimes as 'natural', though patently it is neither) then, it seems to have been argued, the world could have been spared many unnecessary economic

misfortunes. Man-made interference has been disturbing the
self-regulating powers of nature.

It would be unfair to single out these particular pieces of
analytical apparatus from the period before *The General Theory*,
were not so many of the economic attitudes current in the age of
unemployment beyond caricaturing. But they are a reminder of
the dangers in reaching policy conclusions on the hypothesis of a
single rate of interest. In the real world rates run from zero (on
current account balances with banks) to over 20 per cent (the
real cost to the buyer of hire-purchase finance), and the relationship between the intervening rates is determined at any
given time not only by supposed risk of loss or possibility of gain,
but by maturity, marketability, cost of realisation, tax position
and convenience. Changes in the relative position of rates can
give rise to changes in the flow of finance generally, and its
direction into particular types of enterprise. Here is reason for
thinking in neutral terms of relative 'rates of return', in order to
avoid an illusory precision.

Objections to traditional usage can, however, only claim
justification in so far as they prepare the ground for something
more meaningful. An attempt will be made to develop such an
approach in a following chapter. In summary, it goes like this.

First, our daily economic existence is made possible by, as it
were, a fabric of interlocking financial obligations, constantly
maturing, being liquidated, being added to. Such transactions
take time to complete, and may bring related obligations into
being. All these obligations arise out of the uncompleted transactions called for in the course of our normal activities. Every
one of these transactions due for settlement gives rise to an asset
to the one who is entitled to receive and a liability to the one
who is due to pay.

Only a small part of our current transactions are completed
simultaneously. The basic business of earning one's living illus-
trates this: a man receives his wages at the end of the week, but
all through that week his employer has been incurring a mount-
ing liability, and the worker has an increasing asset in what he

is owed. (In passing, it may be observed that this process can pre-date the existence of an acceptable form of money; it applies equally if the wages are due to be paid in kind.)

It follows that we are concerned with the capacity to enter into obligations requiring settlement after an interval of time, and with the ways in which they are settled.

Second, these obligations normally fall to be settled by a process of offset; what we are due to pay is set off against what we are due to receive. There is, as it were, a great cancellation process operated for the most part by the banking system. In theory, this offsetting should only take place when maturing liabilities coincide in time with maturing assets; in practice, the banks are able to bridge intervals by matching obligations and by substituting their own to cover differences in timing.

Third, since payment is made by way of cancellation of assets against liabilities, the essential feature is access to the cancellation system. This can be secured by:

(i)   having immediately available claims in one's favour in respect of which we can instruct the bank (credit balances);

(ii) claims maturing at a later date, or possessions of value, or satisfactory prospects on the strength of which we can persuade the bank to intervene and meet immediate claims on our behalf (bank advances); or

(iii) by having claims or possessions which we can dispose of to other people in exchange for immediate claims which can be used to secure access to the cancellation process (realisable assets).

Fourth, *liquidity* is the capacity for giving access to the cancellation process; liquidity reflects capacity to pay. A credit balance with a bank is completely liquid. Government debt payable on demand or maturing shortly, or a secured debt falling due in the near future, are very nearly so. Other assets are liquid to the extent that they are easily realisable (i.e. exchangeable for immediately maturing claims and easily replaceable). The implications of liquidity are examined later; for immediate purposes it is enough to see it as a quality of infinite gradations representing the ease with which claims and possessions can be used to give access to the banks for purposes of payment.

Fifth, in this concept 'money' in the conventional sense is of secondary importance. Of course an unexpected or induced shortage of cash can in the short run cause anything from inconvenience to chaos according to the circumstances in which it takes place. But in normal conditions this is not an issue.

Where effective intervention can take place is in the cancellation processes operated by the banks: anything which slows down the ease and speed with which assets and liabilities are being set off against each other opens the way to regulating the rate of economic activity.

The central feature of the approach outlined in the five points above is the general view of liquidity as providing access to a cancellation system. Economic activity is founded on some people buying or committing themselves to something for which in due course they will have to settle: that is, on entering into obligations. Liquidity is the capacity to settle obligations, and this in its turn is equivalent to the capacity for entering into them. Liquidity means power to pay.

Where is money in all this? Money, it must be confessed, has by now gone out of the window, and if it crawls back, it is as a supply of convenient counters to be used in settling transactions which it is cumbersome to handle through the banking system.

The substitution of payment-by-cancellation for payment-through-money as the key to the understanding of our 'monetary' processes brings relief to a strange and disturbed series of concepts. It also has very considerable implications (as will be seen in the chapter immediately following). Its justification, however, must lie in how far it can be made to throw light on what is happening. An attempt to apply this liquidity approach to the financial institutions operating in the United Kingdom is undertaken in the three subsequent chapters.

But if it is to justify itself, this concept cannot be confined to the domestic affairs of Britain, as we know full well. So the next step following will be to examine how far it throws light on what can happen on international account. The concluding portion of this book assesses the pressures operating on our financial system and discusses what changes in its machinery we might think of making with advantage.

CHAPTER TWO

Payment and Liquidity

1. *The Structure of Obligations*

One must look at the nature of obligations before turning to the means of settling them.

The financial texture of society is composed of obligations.[1] They are all-pervasive: constantly arising, being replaced, disappearing as they are discharged. They may reflect anything from isolated claims to continuing arrangements. They are of every kind, from sales and purchase of things to replacement or rearrangement of debts.

These obligations have this in common: they represent transactions in part due for later completion. The simultaneous transaction where a bargain is entered into, fulfilled and settled on the spot is of secondary importance if one takes account of the economy as a whole. To a larger extent, transactions take time; one party performs his side of a transaction, and the other his side later on. A simple example is that of a man at his work. He will be paid weekly or monthly. As the week or month goes on the man working is accumulating an increasing claim on his employer which is settled when pay-day comes round. Near the other extreme, a man buys or rents a house, and undertakes to

---

[1] In quantitative terms: the physical assets of the U.K. have been valued (in £ thousand million) at 50 for land, dwellings and buildings, 20 for plant and equipment, 10 for stocks and 4 for consumers' durable goods—total 85. Erected on this base was a financial superstructure of assets/liabilities of some 140 to 150. Figures relate to 1961. (J. Revell, 'The Wealth of the Nation', *Moorgate and Wall Street*, spring 1966.) To complete the picture, in 1961 the Gross National Product was over 24, and the National Income over 22, and we all know that there are over 50 million inhabitants in the U.K.

make regular payments over a period of years. Transactions take time either because their nature requires it, or in response to the choice, convenience or bargaining power of the participants. And transactions which take time involve obligations: in the simplest case, one man is left with a claim which he has to meet to the benefit of another; in a more complicated case—the renting of a house, for example—there is a mutual commitment. One man undertakes to make regular payments, and the other to see that the house is kept in suitable condition.

Particular claims should not be looked at in isolation. From the point of view of the community and of those who compose it, claims are interlocking: you are able to enter into an obligation to render a service or make a payment to someone else because you are sure that others will be doing things or making payments in your favour. The individual knows that he has commitments on the one hand and benefits to come on the other, and he takes the whole picture—his expected receipts and his necessary outgoings, or, in balance-sheet terms, his assets and his liabilities—into account in considering what further transactions he is prepared to enter into.

It is a mistake to regard such an interlocking system of obligations as being entirely dependent on the existence of a monetary system. In a simple form we can even envisage it in a world of barter. On pay-day the employer is called on to provide a supply of foodstuffs and other essential commodities in agreed amounts. The employed may in his turn be called on to pass on some of these commodities in payment of the services he has been receiving in the interval, and so on. If we can imagine an effective barter economy where bargains are struck on the basis of the various goods as they become available, a network of obligations must be a necessary part of it.

Indeed, one can carry the argument further, and discover processes at work corresponding to those in a monetary economy. The businessman in a monetary economy who miscalculates will not have enough in the bank to pay his workmen at the end of the week. His fellow who has been overtrading in a barter economy will not have enough goods to go round to honour the obligations he has entered into. Nor is the parallel of running out of liquid cash the only one. Inflation, in the commonplace sense of 'too much money chasing too few goods', becomes 'too many claims in terms of goods chasing too few goods'—resulting, in the barter society, in the inadequate supply of goods having to be allocated by rationing or by force, and expectations being disappointed.

It would therefore be wrong to regard a network of obligations as developing out of the existence of monetary arrangements (though clearly such arrangements enable the scale of obligations to be immeasurably extended). On the contrary, it is the existence of such obligations which gives the opportunity for monetary arrangements, providing both a measure of obligations and the means of settling them, to enter into the picture. What this amounts to is that debts and credits can arise independently of money, though obviously the scope must be very seriously limited in the absence of some more general unit of account.

2. *The Settlement of Obligations*

We settle obligations by making payment. The accepted methods of payment do not remain the same. Settlement in a barter society calls for the handing over of physical goods or the rendering of services. In time this is reinforced and then superseded by the handing over of conventionally acceptable goods of intrinsic value by way of settlement—precious metals, and in due course precious metals in easily identifiable form such as coins. This phase in its turn passes; coins lose their intrinsic value and become counters. In so far as we do make use of coins today, it is for comparatively small transactions. For larger transactions we settle either in acceptable pieces of paper (notes) or use book-keeping entries.

The disappearance of coins of full value is only just fifty years old. In the United Kingdom gold sovereigns were in regular use up to the beginning of the 1914–18 war. Silver coinage continued till a good deal later; the copper content of our pennies and halfpennies still remains, and the coins are inconveniently large. But coinage has quite literally been reduced to small change. The largest coin in use in this country is the half-crown, and its purchasing power is not much more than that of the pre-1914 6d. Yet before 1914 there were in circulation some 5s. and 4s. pieces. The gap has been filled by 10s., £1 and £5 notes, with the tantalising statement on them that the Chief Cashier of the Bank of England promises to pay the bearer on demand the sum of £1 (or whatever it may be). But such notes, like the coins, are in their turn convenient counters for use in commonplace transactions. Aside from weekly wage packets and the smaller household purchases, our more serious business is conducted largely by means of cheques.

Payment in the old sense of an exchange in which something of intrinsic value passes has given way to a process of cancellation. We settle our debts to others by setting them off in turn against debts due to us, or by substituting a further debt due from us to someone else. Our bank balance is a debt due to us from our bank; by cheque we transfer an appropriate part of this to our creditor, so that his bank balance—the debt due to him from his bank—is increased accordingly. But we do not even need a positive bank balance. If our bank agrees, it will be prepared to incur a debt to our creditor in return for an increased debt from us—which is what happens when the manager allows an increase in an overdraft. Here one obligation is substituted for another. Payment has become a gigantic routine of book-keeping and cancellation.

This is not confined to banks. There used to be a piece of business in pantomime which went like this. The chief comic says to the principal boy: 'You owe me half-a-crown.' The principal boy turns to the second comic: 'You owe me half-a-crown.' He in his turn challenges someone else for half-a-crown. The last person challenged completes the circle, demanding half-a-crown from the chief comic. Everybody present owes and is owed half-a-crown. The circle may be complete, but no one has half-a-crown.

The chief comic is a man of resource. He turns to the conductor of the orchestra and persuades the maestro to produce half-a-crown, to be repaid forthwith. The half-a-crown passes from the chief comic to the last in line and then to the next and round the circle till it comes back to the chief comic. He returns it with a flourish to the maestro. At any rate everybody is out of debt, even though they still have not got half-a-crown between them.

Such a story seems to demand a moral. Suppose the conductor had not had half-a-crown. The same result could have been achieved by passing a sixpence round the group five times. A dud half-crown would have done the trick. Indeed, if there had been a hypnotist on the programme, an imagined half-crown could have settled all those debts. Or perhaps even a packet of ten cigarettes, if it went round unopened. The possibility of restraining music-hall artistes from getting into debt by constricting the means of payment is not all that some might have hoped.

We are all less and less concerned with 'having money' in a narrow sense. What matters is access to money, or—more exactly—access to means of payment, that is to the machinery of cancellation. We have such access if we have a balance at a bank, or are entitled to borrow from a bank, or have assets which can conveniently be cashed or sold or pledged as security in such a way as to build up a balance at a bank. When we sell or encash assets we are paid for them, and the bank has no say in what we do with the proceeds. In so far as we want to make payment by means of borrowing from a bank (with or without pledging assets), this is a matter on which our bank has a decision to make. Our overriding purpose is to maintain the facility for payment at our bank on the scale called for by the commitments we expect to have to meet.

The components in this process are first, the liquidity of our assets, in the sense of the ease with which they can be turned into, or used as a basis for, credits at a bank available for making payment; and second, our expected liabilities—that is the extent and timing of the payments which we may be called upon to make. Our decisions about the character and amount of the assets which we hold will be determined by what we have already, and what we expect in the way of forthcoming receipts and outgoings. If we look like being unable to meet the claims upon us, we take steps to alter the character of our assets or to reduce the scale on which we are entering into commitments— or we find ourselves in trouble.

3. *Assets and Liabilities*

Every financial obligation has two sides. For the beneficiary it is an asset, entitling him to receive the original amount due, and possibly something further in respect of the time the claim was outstanding. For the man who is due to pay, it is a liability to be met at due date in full, together with interest and other charges.

The extent to which people can at any time add to their obligations will depend on their ability so to match their assets and liabilities that their prospective liquid resources, in terms of capacity to draw on their bank account, remain sufficient to cover prospective outgoings. This preoccupation with liquidity is fundamental. On the one hand it is profitable to enter into transactions (which in their turn may give rise to further trans-actions) on which settlement comes later; on the other, assets and liabilities must be so interlocked that there is no failure to meet obligations. Hence preoccupation with the cash position, and such claims as can easily be turned into cash, using cash in the sense of ability to make payments by a convenient and recognised process—normally out of a bank account.

One can look at accumulations of wealth as being arranged in a kind of spectrum: at one end cash needed for working purposes; then various investments quickly realisable or suitable as security for borrowings should unforeseen emergencies or attractive opportunities make an increase in bank facilities necessary; then securities less easily realisable but likely to maintain their value in the long run; then other securities offering a higher (but less certain) return or a good prospect of capital appreciation; and at the other extreme all kinds of investments of a much more unpredictable character. Against such a background it is easier to see how the size of the bank balance which someone holds is determined not only in the light of expected income and outgoings, but also by the ease with which other assets can be turned into cash should need arise.

When the balance at the bank is larger than we need, we put the excess to work by investing it to bring in a return, that is, by adding to our income-earning assets. How large a return will depend on the conditions we are prepared to accept for reducing the balance at the bank. If we want to be able to turn assets back into cash quickly should it be necessary, we must only lend for short periods and to reliable borrowers. A balance in the Post Office Savings Bank brings in only $2\frac{1}{2}$ per cent and a deposit account with a bank, subject to seven days' notice, will often bring in little more (though we know well enough that there are periods when the rate can rise well above this). On the other hand, if we are prepared to commit ourselves for long periods ahead, the rate of return can be considerably larger.

But the higher interest to be earned on long-term lending is compensation for disadvantages which arise even where the borrower is beyond question able to repay.

In the first place, it may be impossible to realise the investment and turn it into cash except at a loss. There is no obligation on the borrower to repay (as long as interest payments are kept up) until the agreed date a long time ahead. After the original loan was made, rates of interest generally may have risen. New investors, invited to take over existing investments, will reduce the amount they are prepared to pay if they can get the higher return on later investments bearing a higher rate of interest. The holder of a claim will therefore have to take a loss in the amount he receives in pounds if he is not prepared to keep the claim till maturity. The danger is that of a rise in the rate of interest after an investment has been made.

The other major disadvantage is that of rising prices. A right to receive a fixed number of pounds at regular intervals becomes less attractive if, as a result of rising prices, the purchasing power of the pound is diminishing. So there is this second danger, that of inflation: the diminishing amount of goods and services which can be purchased as time goes on with a given number of pounds.

Finally there is the cost involved in making certain long-term investments, which may be considerable.

An investor with wealth at his disposal will not confine himself to fixed-interest lending but will also distribute his wealth between other types of asset. As a private citizen he may decide, if he wishes to protect himself from higher prices, to buy his house (which will increase in value if prices rise) or precious objects such as jewels or pictures. If he is seeking an income and not just a steady increase in the value of objects he possesses, it is open to him to buy an interest in a business or a range of businesses, which he can do most simply by acquiring ordinary shares quoted on the Stock Exchange. This means that, instead of being entitled to a fixed return on his investment, he will receive dividends paid out of the profits that the company is making. If prices are rising, the dividends paid by a prosperous company may be expected to increase, so that the loss in purchasing power of a currency will be compensated through the larger amounts paid out in dividends at a time when in general higher prices should mean higher profits.

Equity holdings should reflect the expansion of the economy, but they have their own attendant risks. The economy has its ups and downs, and in moments of reduced activity equity holdings will be lower in value and may entail a loss if they have to be realised in order to restore liquidity. Or the fortunes of a particular company may be affected adversely by circumstances peculiar to it. But against these risks there is the favourable fact that in general good ordinary shares tend to increase in value over the years as the business concerned expands, and a sensible and well-spread selection should lead to a substantial gain.

It is against such a background that investors add to their holdings. The spectrum of assets runs from cash through investments which are modest in return but easily turned into cash without loss to others where the promise of substantial gain entails risks and some disadvantages.

With business undertakings the position is not dissimilar to that of individuals, but is enormously greater in scale. A balance-sheet will show cash and money with the bankers as a small—sometimes very small—proportion of assets. Notes and coin will be quite negligible; companies (apart from financial institutions) have little need of them except on pay-day, when they will be collected from the bank and paid out with as small an interval as possible. The balance at the bank will vary from season to season. In addition to seasonal fluctuations in the business done, provision will have to be made for dividend and tax payments as they fall due.

But a business undertaking which carries excessive amounts in physical cash or balances at the bank is open to the criticism that it is wasting opportunities; the money should be more actively employed, either in the business or in more profitable use outside it. If the financial arrangements of an undertaking are well thought out, any temporary needs for cash, whether for the wages bill at the end of the week, or for regular dividend payments, or for large tax payments, or for seasonal purchases of materials, might be met economically by special arrangement for temporary borrowing from banks or otherwise, and then paid off out of receipts as they accrue. The object would be to keep the amount of idle finance at a minimum.

The guiding consideration is thus not the absolute size of the bank balance but the certainty that necessary additional amounts can be obtained for short periods. It follows that those in charge of an undertaking will be sensitive above all to any change in the possibility of making temporary arrangements to replenish the bank balance as required. A business must pay attention to its liquidity position. A tightening-up which reduces this capacity to borrow and makes borrowing more difficult is therefore of special concern to an enterprise which depends on meeting its obligations promptly. If the pressure is at all serious, it must affect the decisions made by the management who— unable to borrow as much as they would like—have to build up balances in advance out of current income as it comes in. This may have to be done by cuts in various types of expenditure which would otherwise have taken place. If a company is over-trading and fails to meet some obligations, the knowledge will spread, other demands for payment will be accelerated, and it may be in real trouble.

The position of the private individual is, of course, much the same. Told by his bank manager that overdraft facilities will be given less freely, he will decide to postpone redecorating his house or buying the new car till the following year. It should be noted that here also (as in the case of the business undertaking) the more serious threat is the scale on which the borrowings will be allowed, rather than the fact that they may cost more.

4. Liquidity and Insolvency

One has to distinguish between a failure of liquidity on the one hand, and insolvency. The former means inability to meet payments as they fall due; the latter, that liabilities exceed assets, with no prospect of continuing in business at a profit.

A failure of liquidity takes the form of the exhaustion of means of payment. For the individual, it means not enough money in the bank to meet the bills, and proceedings being started in the courts. For a business, it means not enough in the bank to provide the cash to pay wages at the end of the week. Or again, a refusal of suppliers of materials or components to make further deliveries till outstanding bills have been met, and a stoppage of production in consequence.

Though an undertaking has for the moment come to a stop through lack of money, it it not necessarily running at a loss. On the contrary, it may have been too successful, and its managers lacking in caution. They may have taken on far more profitable business than they could handle given that they have to make large payments to workpeople and suppliers at the outset, but are paid only after an appreciable delay. If they have failed to make proper arrangements for working capital, for example failing to persuade their bank manager or to secure alternative financial support, they reach a crisis. Work comes to a standstill, or creditors take over. This is a failure of finance, the consequence of entering into obligations on a scale and of a type beyond what the liquidity position of the undertaking can take care of. If the business is ultimately sound and profitable, the trouble being that it has been conducted rather wildly, the undertaking could be rescued and put on its feet and continue to operate. The receiver, or whoever had been put in charge to sort out the mess, might be successful in getting in the money owed to the business and finding further finance. The outcome then might be enough both to meet claims of creditors in due course and yield a surplus, enabling activities to be carried on. In such a case there is a failure of liquidity; but insolvency has been avoided.

In other frequent cases a failure of liquidity is only a prelude to insolvency. But there is a third type where a company which is insolvent may still have adequate liquid assets for the time being. A business in a bad way may see demand for its output falling rapidly. But for some time amounts coming to it from past sales when trade was better may be providing it with plentiful cash. It may be selling currently at a loss without being pressed for money. If this is so, it is only a question of time. If nothing is done, sooner or later the assets will be dissipated, and if the receiver is not called in early enough, the subsequent liquidation will not provide enough to cover the liabilities.

The parallel in the case of individuals is that of the Bankruptcy Court. A man may make a mess of his financial affairs, and yet in the end when things have been sorted out will be able to pay 20s. in the £. This will be his liquidity crisis. On the other hand, he may be unable to pay off his creditors and will be made bankrupt.

It should be noted that a failure of liquidity can involve severe penalties, even when liquidation can be avoided. In the first place, it will be difficult to avoid a stoppage, or at any rate a sharp cutting-back of activity, until rescue money can be obtained. This hold-up will of itself contribute to losses. Second, the price of rescue money may be very unfavourable to the existing proprietors. They may be ousted and the benefits of the reconstruction (and the underlying value of the business) may in whole or in part go to their successors. Third, the impression of failure may in fact bring about that very failure not because the immediate position was beyond repair, but because the fear created among creditors and customers leads to such loss of goodwill and such pressure that the business cannot be restarted and ultimately becomes insolvent.

5. *Liquidity and the Concept of Money*

The present approach in terms of liquidity has avoided the use of the term 'money'. It starts from the existence of a network of obligations constantly being modified by the disappearance of old obligations and the coming of new ones; it centres on the capacity of the obligations to be set off one against another. Where does money fit into the liquidity approach?

Traditional definitions of money saw its functions as that of a unit of account, a medium of exchange and a store of value.

As long as gold sovereigns were in general circulation—up to 1914—the pound sterling had an embodiment to which such definitions could be related. Accounts kept in pounds were accounts the balances on which could be settled in gold sovereigns, even if often they were not; hence the unit of account. As regards the medium of exchange, gold sovereigns did pass from hand to hand where settlement was made on the spot. Lastly, gold sovereigns could be stored away in a safe place and accumulated for future use: indeed, were a sensible way of holding a reserve of wealth against unexpected needs or unforeseen emergencies.

But we are faced with a very different picture now that the physical value of coins has gone.

Unit of account? This remains up to a point: we work in pounds, just as others work in dollars or francs or pesetas. But even here things are changing before our eyes. In a world of rising prices we encounter statistics—indeed we cannot avoid using some statistics—which give figures expressed in terms of pounds subject to the qualification of 'at 1958 prices'. Contracts have in them revaluation provisions. Accounting experts argue whether capital depreciation should be based not on historic cost but on replacement. So although our accounting continues in sterling or other currencies, it might be preferable to think of this function of money as being 'the measure of indebtedness' rather than unit of account.

Medium of exchange? This had meaning before coins of physical value had disappeared. The bits of paper or pieces of metal which we carry around in our pockets have no intrinsic value as such. The volume of coins or notes in circulation is in practice determined by the public alone; no one any longer expects monetary policy to be exerted through the creation of a shortage of physical cash. The transfer of bank credit is a different matter: that in fact is the method by which most large transactions are settled. But even here there are obstacles to identifying bank credit with 'money'. The volume of bank deposits shown in the statistics—even if confined to the bank deposits on current account—is not the fixed and immutable amount on which we operate by cheque; we operate on deposits plus unused overdraft facilities or advance limits which are often only defined in general terms. To this point we return in a moment.

Money as a store of value? This made sense when we put gold sovereigns aside and locked them in a safe. But apart from relatively small amounts held for convenience (and larger amounts illicitly obtained), no one has a rational inducement to hold notes in quantity for savings purposes. The needs of a store of value would be better met through interest-earning deposit accounts and relatively liquid assets such as savings certificates or National Development Bonds, to stop short of the inclusion of more venturesome forms of investment which would meet the needs of storing wealth, or through the holding of physical objects of value themselves.

We must now turn back to the previous proposition, that the concept of money as a medium of exchange is no longer meaningful. What does this imply, and should we not be able to put something more meaningful in its place? Our argument must in essence be based on the proposition that accepted means of payment are not strictly limited in quantity. What happens is that they are more or less hard to come by. This means that the position can change in quality. This is what happens when we cease thinking in terms of money which is fixed in amount and think in terms of liquidity instead. A financial writer can speak of 'an excess of liquidity'. The phrase may be cumbersome but it is fair enough. It expresses the view that the position in the financial markets or wherever it may be is such as to predispose people into entering into new commitments on what in the event may prove an excessive scale. It implies that people will be examining their financial position—what they owe and are owed, what they expect to come in and go out, their ability to realise assets if required—and they find the position sufficiently assuring to go in for new expenditures, new commitments, new enterprises. The extent to which they will do so is not mathematically predetermined, but the underlying conditions are unmistakable.

If one substitutes for that 'too much liquidity' the simpler English of 'too much money', a misleading impression at once intervenes. In fact we cannot find anything specific which corresponds to 'money' in the sense that that phrase requires it. We do not mean that there is too much physical cash in circulation; if there were it would go back to the banks. The volume of bank balances outstanding at any one time is not a properly relevant figure. At best we might try to work something out on a basis which also includes unused credit facilities at the banks and argue from that and say that these are excessive. However, it is impossible to arrive at even an approximate total. Many limits are designed to be used in sequence: the farmer's overdraft is paid off when the grain merchant's goes up, and to add together unused limits which are not intended for simultaneous use is to bring in double-counting. And this is only one difficulty. There will be many shades of commitment; some potential commitments may never approach reality; the concept of money as being related to a contingent rather than to an actual figure deprives it of coherence. On the other hand to speak of an excessive liquidity gives us something realistic, and avoids the mistake of implying a precision which cannot exist.

This is the objection to methods of analysis based on the old versions of the Quantity Theory of Money. Whether we think in terms of a stock of money turning over so many times on the average during a given period, or whether we take the average amount of cash outstanding as a proportion of the National Income during a year, we are compelled to use the assumption of a measurable amount of 'cash'. Such a hypothesis removes the argument that much further from reality. The looser concept of liquidity as applying to a wide range of assets is more illuminating on what is really involved.

This is not to deny that the banking system as a whole is in a position to influence the volume of deposits held with it. Banks can at any moment lend more (if they relax standards to attract the needed borrowers) or buy more securities (if going rates are acceptable). This will increase total deposits. Or they can reduce their lending and sell securities which will draw down deposits. But the decision of the banks to increase or decrease the volume of deposits standing to the credit of their account-holders is only the first stage in a process; what really matters is how the account-holders will themselves reassess their positions and make adjustments in the structure of their assets and liabilities. It is this which will call for decisions to spend or invest, to enter into new obligations or to cut back on the scale of commitments.

6. *The Return on Assets and the Concept of Interest*

The plea so far is for thinking in terms of liquidity, and for avoiding the use of a concept of money which assumes that the amount of it in existence can be quantitatively measured. There is an equally strong case against the concept of a generalised rate of interest, and displacing it in favour of an approach in terms of the different returns to be expected from different classes of asset, and the causes and effects of divergence between them.

The concept of a single rate of interest is a hypothesis based on the rate of return which will emerge in a simplified situation with the other factors given. It has its limited uses to illustrate an argument. But it has the misfortune to resemble the long-term rate of interest on Government borrowing, and from this it is only a short step to equate the theoretical rate of interest with the return on gilt-edged.

For a great many purposes such a simplification is illegiti-mate. Where we are concerned with a spectrum of assets giving different returns, these returns will not follow any general average but will have changing relationships with each other. Various rates are likely to move in different directions as situations change. To illustrate:

(i) Short- and long-term interest rates, even where gilt-edged are concerned, will move in different directions according to changes in liquidity conditions: for example, when, to make themselves more liquid, on balance people want to increase their holdings of short-term securities and reduce their long-term holdings, short-term rates will fall and long-term rise.

(ii) People do not only hold fixed-interest securities; on the contrary, they will look to their holdings of equities in the hope of securing capital appreciation and protecting themselves against rising prices, and the relationship between the running yield on equities and that on fixed-interest securities will fluctuate. Fixed-interest rates can at the same time be described as either high or low according to whether allowance is made for changes in the purchasing power of money.

(iii) The risk of loss (of a cut or cessation of dividends, or of default on fixed-interest obligations) must be taken into account. This will vary both generally from time to time as economic conditions change, and will also affect particular obligations according to particular circumstances.

(iv) The cost of realisation will vary as between investments.

(v) The taxation position will vary as between different assets and also as between different holders. We shall see that this can have far-reaching consequences.

It is true that, comparing one point of time with another, we can broadly say that the return to be obtained from the acquiring of a representative range of assets was by and large greater or smaller in the earlier or later period. But for most purposes we are compelled to work in terms of a series of returns, subject to different conditions and relating to different types of asset whose values may move up and down for reasons which may be quite different from each other.

7. Implications of Liquidity

Here it may be convenient to summarise the approach in terms of liquidity set out in the previous pages.[1] The main features are these:

(1) We start with the existence of an interlocking network of financial obligations of every sort and kind. Some are constantly disappearing as they are discharged. New commitments are constantly giving rise to new obligations in their place.

(2) These financial obligations interlock, first, because what one man is due to pay another is due to receive. One man's liability is another man's asset, and vice versa. Everyone— individual and business institution—is due both to pay and to receive, and so has both assets and liabilities. In the second place many of the obligations involve consequential obligations arising from them.

(3) Assets can be arranged in an order to reflect the extent to which they are immediately or easily available to make payment at one extreme, and realisable only with great difficulty at the other. The distribution between types of assets will be dictated by contradictory considerations: on the one hand resources in a liquid or near-liquid form are a protection against the danger of inability to pay, and leave scope for embarking on new commitments should opportunities present themselves; on the other, the longer-term and less liquid assets offer a higher

[1] The position here is a development of that in A. T. K. Grant, *A Study of the Capital Market* (Macmillan, 1937), in particular pp. 16–23. It would seem to be close to that adopted by the Radcliffe Committee (*Report of the Committee on the Working of the Monetary System*, Cmd. 827, 1959), in particular paras. 389–93. The main difference is that the present approach treats liquidity in terms of capacity to enter into obligations without enlisting the concept of money substitutes, which is rejected on the ground that it is meaningless to think of substitutes for the means of payment. Hence the concept of cancellation. The present writer would also like to acknowledge the influence of ideas from Sir John Hicks (in particular 'A Suggestion for Simplifying the Theory of Money', *Economica*, February 1935), and Professor R. S. Sayers.

rate of return. Hence the spectrum of assets running from liquid and unremunerative bank balances at one end through various intermediate stages to permanent assets with a range of high returns at the other.

(4) The way in which assets will be allocated between the extremes will be determined by the timing of expected liabilities and the prospect of future income arising to reinforce existing assets as payment falls due. Those of limited means, with regular living expenses to meet and emergencies to be prepared for, and an income largely earned, will ultimately have to keep wealth in relatively liquid form. The rich man can have more room for manœuvre because he can afford to tie it up more profitably but more permanently, knowing that he need not be called on to use it to make unavoidable payments in a hurry. The business undertaking will be watching its figures to see that it is using its capital effectively without at the same time running the risk of being embarrassed by a shortage of funds for necessary payments.

(5) Payment is made

    (a) in physical cash—notes and coin no longer having any intrinsic value—when it comes to the payment of wages, and current purchases in moderate amounts.

    Larger payments are made

    (b) in effect by a process of offsetting liquid assets against current liabilities through the mechanism of the banks. The liquidity of an asset can be looked on as the capacity it has for giving access to this facility: a liquid asset takes the form of a balance at a bank, or something suitable as security for a loan from a bank, or something which can be conveniently disposed of and turned into a balance at a bank.

(6) This liquidity approach leaves—deliberately—the concept of money in a subsidiary role. The amount of notes and cash in circulation is dictated by current requirements, which must be met. The volume of deposits shown in the bank's

statistics is not directly relevant: in part some of these deposits are inactive, but more important, the possibilities of payment at any given moment of time must include not only actual balances but potential additions such as liquidity makes possible. We are fully entitled to say that at a point of time there is 'excessive liquidity' as long as we do not suggest that we can put an exact figure on it. But we are not entitled to talk of 'too much money' unless it is made absolutely clear that we cannot measure the excess.

This approach, based on the general application of the concept of liquidity, leads directly to a number of matters of consequence.

In the first place, it has been concerned with the facilities for *settling* obligations. Now when we speak of facilities for settling obligations, we are at one and the same time discussing facilities for *entering into* them. We are thus taken straight to the heart of the financial-economic problem, since it is through decisions on whether or not to embark on new transactions that effective demand is determined.

Second, this approach leaves in full view one important respect in which there is a lack of symmetry: there is no reason to assume that when a payment is made from A to B, the subtraction from the liquidity (i.e. capacity for entering into further obligations) of A is balanced by the addition to the liquidity of B; it may be greater or less, but it need not correspond. Nor is it an answer to say that while this is true of particular payments taken in isolation, the effect of the large number of payments at any one time is to cancel out any differences for practical purposes. But why should it? The tide may be running from rich to poor, or vice versa, or from one area to another; but the addition to the liquidity of the recipients need not correspond to the subtraction of liquidity in the case of those who buy even though the money totals are one and the same. This asymmetry can apply not only to payments within countries, but to payments between countries, and in both cases the consequences can be important.

The third aspect bears on methods of control by monetary authorities. When a given liquidity structure is thought to be stimulating excessive demand, the imposition of monetary restraints must depend on an impact effect if it is to fulfil an immediate purpose. Restraints which are imposed without warning or at short notice do have an effect on a given situation—in certain circumstances even an effect verging on the dangerous. With warning, their consequences may be anticipated and their effectiveness nullified. Liquidity structures are adaptable: given enough time, new techniques and institutions will evolve types of obligation which escape the restraints.

Fourth, we have taken note of the passing away of money in the old sense of coins of intrinsic value. It is not enough to leave it at that. Is this a change in degree or a change in kind? An answer to this question is of more than historical interest the moment that we move outside a few of the leading industrialised countries. After all, nearly all the world's newly-mined gold is going into hoards and not into the vaults of the central banks. This must be expected to have consequences.

The last three aspects discussed—the second, third and fourth as they are set out above—deal with matters which will have to be explored and argued much more fully.

There is one particular advantage of the liquidity approach, of which we shall avail ourselves. Its concept of assets and liabilities ranged in order—whether we think in terms of a balance-sheet or a spectrum—provides a method by which we can start to examine financial institutions as working entities. Banks, like private citizens, owe and are owed. Why—and on what scale—do people lend to banks? What inducements can the banks offer? How do they compare with their rivals who want to borrow from the general public?

We begin by examining banks and other financial intermediaries first in their role as debtors and then as creditors.

CHAPTER THREE

Banks and Intermediaries as Borrowers

1. *The System in Outline*

The three chapters which follow deal with the central parts of the financial machine. The first is concerned with the banks (and other financial institutions) in their capacity as borrowers: that is, with the process by which they acquire and hold the deposits placed with them. The next turns to the asset side, to see how they operate as lenders and how they employ their funds in changing circumstances. The third (under the heading of 'The Mechanics of Control') brings the two sides together to show their interaction, and to relate this both to the financing of the public sector and to the working of the economy as a whole.

It may be convenient to begin by setting out shortly the main features of the financial structure.

An observer from overseas, in England for the first time, might be struck by three aspects of our financial system. He could be agreeably impressed by the comprehensiveness of the services offered to him for his immediate purposes. The great banking chains cover most of the country. Not only is the country well supplied with banks, but they are much used and easy to deal with. Service is quick and informal and—in spite of the competing facilities—much the same in whichever bank he may go to.

The observer's second impression could leave him puzzled. It is the contrast between the facilities offered to the public and the self-imposed limitations on the scope of the work which the banks themselves undertake. They confine themselves rather rigidly to the making of payments (in providing facilities for which they are competing ferociously with each other) and the borrowing and lending of money, and though they provide wider services for the benefit of their customers they do much of this through independent institutions. For housing loans they will provide an introduction to a building society. If it is a question of buying or selling securities, they will utilise the services of a stockbroker. They do not choose to participate in the ownership of business. Nor do banks usually play much direct part in placing new public issues of capital, beyond collecting the subscriptions when they come in. They are helpful and knowledgeable on all these matters, but the actual responsibility is left to the independent specialist. Taking the system as a whole, a considerable and increasing element of competition is accompanied by a segregation of function. A large range of specialist institutions is maintained and rewarded for doing particular jobs.

The third impression which could be left with the visitor is that most of these specialist facilities are concentrated on London, and that many of them originated or are involved in commerce and investment connected with overseas. If he visits the City the evidence will be all around him. Conversely—the Stock Exchange apart—institutions financing domestic production will not be easy for him to find, and when discovered would seem modest and unambitious.

In general, the conventional financial services needed by the public are widespread and adequate. Alongside the bank branches, representing largely the 'Big Five' banking chains but also smaller banks in various parts of the country, are an efficient (and developing) Post Office Savings Bank system, a network of Trustee Savings Banks, another network of building societies, and to supplement these a number of insurance companies offering life assurance and related savings benefits, concentrating on London but well represented elsewhere. To these must be added a system for buying and selling securities, centred on the London Stock Exchange and supported by local stock exchanges in provincial centres.

All these compete for the savings of the public. But the banks and the building societies have another side to their activities: they are also prepared to lend as well as to borrow. Other financial help is available to the public for the purchase by instalments of motor vehicles and durable household goods, a credit system provided by finance houses but often administered in the first instance through the suppliers of goods themselves.

Such is the range of institutions which caters for the public. More remarkable, perhaps, are the institutions with which the general public comes in contact less frequently.

The most unusual of the special financial features of London is the existence of the discount market, a buffer between the commercial banks and the Bank of England. In other countries the main commercial banks keep accounts with the central bank, and look to this bank for facilities to replenish those accounts should occasion arise. While the Bank of England holds the accounts of the banks, it does not normally allow direct borrowing. When the banks wish to replenish their balances at the Bank, they do so through the discount market. This consists of a number of financial houses with limited capital of their own who trade in Treasury bills, short-term Government bonds and commercial paper. They borrow money on short term from the banks and other large lenders with immediately available funds, and they use these in buying short-term paper of the kinds mentioned. This they sell to financial institutions who have need of assets maturing at particular times.

The discount market is therefore maintaining a pool of short-term paper, which is regularly being replenished, in particular from the weekly offer of Treasury bills. This pool is dependent on the short-term money lent by the banks and others. If the banks require to build up their balances with the Bank of England, in the normal way they recall funds lent to the discount market, and the discount houses—if they are short—will be forced to go to the Bank of England and sell, or borrow against, their holdings of these short-term obligations to get money from the Bank to repay the banks. Instead of the commercial banks borrowing from the Bank or selling assets to it direct, the traditional chain of events is that the banks by recalling funds force the discount market to look to the Bank to replace the money. The borrowing takes place just as it might elsewhere, but indirectly through a third party.

The segregation of functions—of independent institutions rewarded for doing specified jobs—runs very deep in the structure of the City of London. A particularly important group is that of what might still be described to the foreign observer as the big private banks, though in form the majority of them have by now become public companies. The largest of them are at the same time merchant banks[1] (because of their connections overseas and their origin as merchants engaged in foreign trade), accepting houses (because of their provision of lines of credit against which bills can be drawn for purchases of goods at home or overseas), issuing houses (because of their part in organising and underwriting loans and issues of capital to be dealt in on the Stock Exchange) and financial advisers (because of their experience in managing investments, tapping sources of capital and in promoting mergers and dealing with questions of company finance generally). Although they have command of considerable resources from the fortunes of those with whom they originated and their associates, they are in essence intermediaries engaged in reselling the bills they have guaranteed and floating the securities which they have organised. In the past they had great influence and standing in the City because of their overseas connections; latterly changes in the character of foreign trading have reduced their number and tended to make them broaden their interests.

The theme of overseas connections keeps on recurring. It is

[1] 'Merchant bank' is a general term covering a considerable number of financial houses. 'Accepting houses' refers to members of the Accepting Houses Committee, of whom there were eighteen when the Radcliffe Committee took evidence; there were fifty-seven members of the Issuing Houses Committee. There is thus an overlap, with accepting houses the most exclusive category.

manifest in the next category, that of the overseas banks, of whom a great number are represented in London. This covers not only British banks such as the Bank of London and South America, or the Hongkong and Shanghai Banking Corporation, but also many Commonwealth and foreign banks with branches in London. The international connection is further shown in the insurance services provided overseas from London, and shipping and all that goes with it. To this must be added the activity connected with commodities. Gold, tin, copper, rubber, tea and diamonds are not produced in England. But they are dealt with and/or financed from and/or organised and managed from London.

In present circumstances much of this suggests the past. It has about it a flavour of survival—of highly active survival, but of survival nevertheless. And this impression is heightened by a contrast: the relative unimportance of specialised institutions linking finance with the domestic economy.

There are no great agricultural banks, no industrial banks bound up with textiles or the steel or chemical industries.

Between the commercial banking system providing short-term loans on fixed terms and the Stock Exchange market in securities there is a hiatus. A search could discover an Agricultural Mortgage Corporation for the farmers; a Finance Corporation for Industry provides some capital (rather by way of a lender of last resort) for the larger industries; there is an Industrial and Commercial Finance Corporation which provides finance for the development of the smaller expanding companies. But the list of such institutions in this domestic field is short, and they do not compare, in number or standing, with the institutions whose main concern is in the overseas field. The Government—in the past reluctantly, now more willingly—has been forced to try to make the financial prospects of domestic industry more attractive by means of subsidies and investment incentives. It also provides finance itself for power and communications. But the foreign observer would be tempted to conclude that while the ordinary citizen is well served, as is the trader at home and especially overseas, the domestic producer receives only limited support from specialist financial institutions.

So much for an introductory view of the system, by way of approach to a closer examination of its working.

2. *The Allocation of Personal Savings*

What motives influence people in disposing of the money they set aside? Banks, savings banks, building societies, life assurance companies, the Stock Exchange and the Government are all in competition for the savings of the public. Between them they offer a wide range of inducements and opportunities. What determines the scale and direction of savings between these various outlets?

One can see the attractions for people who put their savings into the less liquid assets: buying a house, agreeing to pay premiums on an insurance policy, or buying securities either directly through the Stock Exchange or indirectly through unit trusts. They have the prospect of a higher return, or of ultimate gain. Against this, others may prefer the certainty of being paid regularly without any risk of loss. It is at the liquid end of the spectrum, where the price of easy availability is that returns are usually lower and sometimes negligible, that the inducements are harder to understand.

This liquid end is not confined to accounts with banks. Building societies take deposits; so do the Post Office and Trustee Savings Banks; and finally Savings Certificates and similar investments on offer by the Government also provide a high degree of liquidity.

The choice between these several outlets must clearly be determined by the interaction of profitability and convenience. Accordingly, what they offer is set out in tabular form on pages 48–9.

The first four outlets—those provided by banks, building

societies and finance houses—belong to the private sector of the economy. The remaining six are in effect governmental, though the Trustee Savings Banks are usually treated as participants in the financial world in their own right in respect of their invest- ment departments. All funds coming to these six outlets are put at the disposal of the Government, except for a substantial portion of funds in the investment departments of the Trustee Savings Banks which are lent to local authorities. In addition, a part of the funds at the disposal of the institutions in the private sector also serve to provide finance for government; this applies in particular to the banks.

All these outlets provide a high degree of liquidity to their depositors. The institutions are accessible; the money is safe; it is quickly available and in full; and there is no charge for put- ting in or drawing out.

On the score of accessibility, banks and post offices (through which the Government savings facilities mentioned are all available) have their network spread all over the country. Building societies and Trustee Savings Banks are also widely diffused and represented in all large centres. The finance houses are rather more difficult to contact, and their appeal to the smaller investor is more limited. As regards safety, there is no risk of the institutions taking in savings being unable to pay, subject to the proviso that, in speaking of building societies and hire-purchase finance houses, we are concerned only with institutions of standing.

As regards availability, for the most part repayment can be secured in full on demand or short notice, and even where a longer period of notice has been formally agreed, earlier pay- ment can often be secured provided the depositor is prepared to forgo some interest. The act of investment does not involve the depositor in any cost, and in this respect is different from the Stock Exchange, with its spread between buying and selling prices, as well as brokers' charges and stamp duty. The require- ments of liquidity are well satisfied in respect of all these outlets.

The inducements vary. Some of them are not related to a

Outlets for Liquid Savings (31 May 1967; bank rate 5½ per cent)

	Scale (£ million)	Availability	Return	Notes
Clearing Banks:				
1. Current accounts	5,000	On demand.	None.	12,000 branches. Network for making payments; borrowing facilities; other banking services.
2. Deposit (time) accounts	3,500	7 days' notice.	2% below bank rate: currently 3½%. (See also note below.)	
3. Building societies	5,580 assets at end 1965.	Prescribed periods of notice; not less than one month. In practice withdrawals often allowed on application.	Varying: currently 4¼%, free of income tax but not surtax.	Limit of £5,000 per person per society.
4. Hire-purchase	1,100 assets mid-1966.	3 months notice or more, sometimes with concessions for small withdrawals.	Varying: more for longer notices or larger amounts. 3 and 6 months money would be somewhat above bank rate.	A fair amount of personal deposits attracted by relatively high rates, but main sources of finance from institutions.
Trustee Savings Banks:				
5. Ordinary	1,050	On demand.	2½%. First £15 of interest free of income tax but not surtax.	1,350 offices. Limit of £5,000 per person. Also cheque facilities in respect of non-interest-bearing current accounts.
6. Investment	1,100	Usually on one month's notice, but higher return if longer notice agreed.	Around 5½%, but varies.	£5,000 limit per depositor.

	Deposits	Notice	Interest	Conditions
7. Post Office	1,800 deposits mid-1966.	On demand.	2½%. First £15 of interest free of income tax but not surtax. (See also note below.)	Deposit and withdrawal facilities available at 20,000 post offices. £5,000 limit per depositor.
8. Savings Certificates (12th Issue)	—	On application.	Approx. 5% if held for 5 years; less if cashed earlier. Free of income tax and surtax.	Maximum holding £750.
9. 5½% National Development Bonds	—	One month's notice.	5½% subject to tax but paid without deduction, plus 2% on final redemption.	Redeemable after 5 years. Maximum holding £2,500.
10. Premium Savings Bonds (Series B)	—	On application.	4½% distributed in the form of lottery prizes, free of income tax and surtax.	Maximum holding of £1,250. Winners selected by the machine ERNIE.

Note: On (2) (clearing banks' deposit accounts) it should be noted that large deposits with *non-clearing* banks often earn more than 2 per cent below bank rate.

On (7) (Post Office Savings Bank) an alternative Investment Account facility has been introduced offering 5½ per cent on deposits subject to a month's notice but without any tax concession. There is a limit of £5,000.

For comparative purposes the corresponding returns on non-liquid assets were around 6¾ per cent for British Government dated stocks, whether dated stocks calculated to redemption, or the flat yield on Consols; twenty-year company debenture and loan stocks averaged 7·41 per cent; the dividend yield in industrial ordinary shares averaged 5·35 per cent and the earnings yield 7·23 per cent—the last being calculated on gross profit less corporation tax at 40 per cent, other charges and gross preference dividends.

Bank rate had been brought down to 5½ per cent on 4 May 1967.

financial return at all. In the case of banks, the main inducement is access to a large number of services, of which the most
important are the making of payments by cheque or otherwise
and the bank's lending facilities. In addition there are certain
personal services which the banks render their customers:
advice, information, credit-standing references, the preparation
of income-tax returns, and even trustee functions and help in
getting passports. These facilities are being added to, especially
as regards the making of payments and the drawing of money
when account-holders are away from home. The Trustee
Savings Banks provide many of the same facilities as commercial
banks, but do not make loans to their customers. The Post Office
Savings Bank offers one special attraction. It enables every
holder of a Post Office Savings Bank book to draw on his
account at any post office of size over much longer hours than
do the banks; limited amounts can be drawn out on presentation
and larger amounts at quite short notice, even though the post
office approached is in a different part of the country from where
the holder resides.

The main inducement, however, must remain the return
offered by way of interest. Here two features are conspicuous. In
the first place, in the case of all the Government facilities listed
(and also in that of the building societies) the rates are in a
sense preferential so that there are limits, shown in the table, to
how much any single individual may hold. Second—and this to
some extent explains the first—the returns offered are affected
by the tax concessions which the outlets may be able to offer.
Thus:

(a) *Savings Certificates and Premium Bonds* are free of both
income tax and surtax on interest or prizes.
(b) *Building society interest* is paid free of income tax, but the
surtax-payer has to declare and pay surtax on the
grossed-up amount.
(c) *The Post Office Savings Bank and Trustee Savings Banks'
ordinary departments.* Here the first £15 of interest on the

deposits earning 2½ per cent is free of income tax but not surtax, and tax is payable in full on the excess.

(d) *National Development Bonds* are taxable in full, but interest is paid without deduction, which means that those exempt from income tax are not faced with the need to reclaim.

(e) *Banks, hire-purchase finance houses* and the investment departments of the *Trustee Savings Banks* pay interest which is taxable, but the tax is not deducted at source.

It follows from this that the tax position of the investor must largely influence his choice of outlet. Thus the surtax-payer has every inducement (within the limits allowed) to go for Savings Certificates (which offer 5 per cent) and Premium Bonds (where the prize money is equivalent to 4½ per cent), both tax-free. In addition he can save income tax by putting money into building societies, but he has to pay surtax on his interest grossed up: that is the amount on which he pays surtax is more than the amount he actually receives, since notionally there is added to his receipts the amount he has been relieved of paying by the income-tax concession. The income-tax payer at the standard rate also has an inducement to go for the three outlets so far mentioned. On the other hand, someone who pays no tax at all can go for Development Bonds and clear 5½ per cent, and he may be able to get much the same from the investment departments of the Trustee Savings Banks and more from a finance house; it would not pay him to go for the outlets mentioned earlier since tax exemptions have no value for him. Conversely, bank deposit accounts and current Post Office Savings Bank accounts are unattractive to everyone if income only is taken into account, and especially unattractive to those who have to pay tax.

The effective returns from the several kinds of holdings mentioned in this analysis—it is well to bear in mind—derive from a period of 5½ per cent bank rate and conditions of credit squeeze. Bank rate can and does change, and some of these outlets vary the return they offer in accordance with bank rate; others do not change automatically, though they are strongly influenced by it; others respond little if at all.

It follows that there must be changes in the relationship between the several rates of return. Thus with a fall in bank rate we do not see all rates coming down, but some rates down in varying degrees with others unchanged, and the attraction of the several outlets relative to each other will differ.

The change in rates is automatic in the case of the deposit accounts of the clearing banks. Some of the finance houses would tend to follow bank rate fairly closely, while others would aim to stabilise what they were offering as far as they could. The building societies might have to raise rates with a rise in bank rate, in order to attract funds in competition with outlets which put up rates automatically in such instances, but they would do so with some reluctance in view of the complications of increasing the rates charged to their existing borrowers. The action of the investment departments of the Savings Banks would depend on what return the investments they had made were bringing in, and one would expect some change but not an automatic one. An issue of Savings Certificates, once it is on offer, is expected to continue for several years, or at least until there is a reassessment of the general position independent of any one particular change in bank rate. The National Development Bonds on sale across post office counters would be subject to similar considerations.

Changes in relative returns do have their effect on the volume of money coming forward to particular outlets. Consequently when particular Government savings facilities cease to attract an adequate volume of savings, in time more attractive terms may be offered. In the same way when building societies find they are not getting enough funds to enable them to meet the demand for loans, they are driven to improving on what they offer to those who lend to them, at the same time also increasing their charge to borrowers in order to preserve the working margin. Variations in the flow of funds coming forward to the several outlets take place largely in response to the relative position of the various institutions seeking to obtain short-term money from the public.

Some rates do remain unchanged, more or less insulated from differences outside. They are in particular the Post Office Savings Banks and the ordinary departments of the Trustee Savings Banks. Their $2\frac{1}{2}$ per cent, with tax still to be paid by those subject to it, looks a modest return.

It is especially modest in a world of rising prices. Over the last few years prices have been rising every year at an average rate of some $3\frac{1}{2}$ per cent. This means that to maintain the real value of one's holding one must earn at least $3\frac{1}{2}$ per cent clear of tax, which means 6 per cent with tax at the standard rate—and more in the surtax bracket.

Taking this $3\frac{1}{2}$ per cent as a yardstick, it follows that those with funds on current account with the banks, in the ordinary department of a Trustee Savings Bank or in the Post Office Savings Bank are in real terms failing to maintain the value of their holdings. Those with money in Savings Certificates or in Premium Bonds are holding their position with a small surplus. With investments in building societies the income-tax payer is holding his position, but not the surtax-payer. Finance houses would provide the highest return, and this would about enable the income-tax payer to break even, but the investment departments of the Trustee Savings Banks and Development Bonds would hardly do so.

It will be observed that deposit accounts with clearing banks in these circumstances offer $3\frac{1}{2}$ per cent with bank rate at $5\frac{1}{2}$ per cent. In short, only the non-taxpayer (who—charities apart—is less likely to have a bank account anyway) could preserve the real value of his savings by keeping money on deposit. With rising prices, over a large field the return available is not enough to maintain the value of savings. We are running, not to stay where we are, but in order not to fall too far behind. Savings Certificates and Premium Bonds remain the only serious exceptions to these rules, and they are rationed. Liquidity is a privilege which has to be paid for.

At this stage it may be relevant to observe that the present system of taxing fixed-interest obligations must give ground for misgiving. The public sector is a large and continuing borrower. Nevertheless, as we see, lenders to this sector may be liable to pay tax in respect of many Government securities on the whole amount they receive by way of interest even though it is eroded by rising prices. Further, in the event of any recovery of gilt-edged they could become liable to capital-gains tax on any appreciation should they have occasion to dispose of their holdings. It is hard to imagine anything more discouraging to holders of fixed-interest securities; holders of equities are in a favoured position because with rising prices profits and dividends are also likely to rise. The health of the gilt-edged market may not be able to stand the continuation of such treatment, and some modest possibilities of mitigation will be suggested later.

The conclusion to be drawn from this needs some expansion. What it brings out is not only that the real return on liquid investments is low, but that there are very strong forces driving savings towards the less liquid outlets—property, life assurance, unit trusts and the various forms of Stock Exchange investment —which give the benefits of effective participation in the profits which rising prices can bring.

Even this conclusion requires elaboration. The disadvantages of superfluous liquidity in a world of rising prices vary from time to time. The allocation of savings will be affected not only by actual returns, but also by the estimate of future possibilities. People will hesitate to tie up money in a more or less permanent investment if they feel that the risks are likely to grow or values to fall. They may therefore be prepared to hold assets (at a loss) in liquid form if they feel that this puts them in a position for making more favourable investments if an opportunity occurs later. Existing returns and future expectations will be weighed in the balance against each other. The individual allocating his savings will not only be considering his own personal need for liquidity in the light of his own circumstances; he will also be assessing the prospective benefits he might get by changing the timing of his investment decisions.

It remains to apply the above analysis to what has come about following the announcement of anti-inflationary measures—the freeze/squeeze—in the middle of July 1966. The effects of the measures have to be assessed in the light of a contradictory element in the components.

There are three elements: a freeze element, designed to operate directly to keep down prices and incomes; a credit-squeeze element, designed to make it more difficult to get access to funds which might be spent on consumption, on the purchase of securities, on speculation of land or physical stocks, and on non-essential investment; and a tax element, designed to reduce spending power.

The freeze element, in so far as it is successful, can be expected to slow down the rise in prices. To the extent that it does so, it should help the position of fixed-interest securities and go some way towards restoring the confidence in gilt-edged. It follows from the analysis that the less prices rise in the course of the year, the greater the effective return from fixed-interest investment.

The credit-squeeze element in the short run has an opposite effect; reduced lending and the rise in lending rates means a fall in capital values and the creation of uncertainty. Investors in the first instance are discouraged. At a later stage, conditions may improve and this improvement should be accelerated once bank rate can be brought down again. But a possible improvement in the longer term should not disguise the fact that the initial effect was bound to be depressing.

The tax element reinforces the depressing effect. The reduction in purchasing power affects adversely the profits of existing enterprise and the prospects of new enterprise. This effect may be offset to some extent by the concessions favouring new capital investment.

The upshot of these measures is that they are calculated to stop the rise in prices and to release resources which can be absorbed in new investment leading to greater possibilities of expansion. But one cannot assume that the release of resources —mainly human personnel—will be immediately and automatically followed by their reabsorption in the strategic sectors of the economy. Will there be a smooth transition from release to redeployment and expansion while avoiding a fresh impetus to rising prices, or will a more drastic reversal—quite possibly still accompanied by a control of prices and incomes—be needed to reactivate the economy?

The impact effect was to slow down the rise in production more than the rise in prices, though without such measures costs and prices could have moved up very much faster. Some reduction of pressure in the economy was needed. But reactivation also may be necessary; one cannot expect renewed expansion if we are left for any length of time with an inconclusive effect on the upward movement of prices coupled with further discouragement for the gilt-edged market for savings, and a depressing prospect for new investment.

3. *The Temporary Investment of Business Funds*

The investment decisions of the private individual when he distributes his savings between the various outlets open to him are—as we have seen—somewhat intricate in character. Those which arise in running a business involve much larger amounts, but they are more clear-cut.

What follows excludes institutions engaged in finance, since their calculations are based on matching obligations between which there may be narrow margins of return. It is concerned with undertakings which deal with things, whether by way of primary production, manufacture or trade and distribution. Such businesses are mostly concerned with finding funds for their own particular purposes, which are to maintain or enlarge the scale of their production or their trading. A prosperous business, assuming expectations are realised, will in practice be earning a substantial return on its employed capital: 12, 15 or 20 per cent and even more. Further, if it is ripe for expansion, it will be on the lookout for opportunities for enlarging the scale of its operations, whether by physical investment in bricks and mortar or machinery, or by the acquisition of similar or complementary businesses. The motive behind expansion is the prospect of being able to employ to good account in its own field the further resources accruing to it, and the return it will expect from this should be substantially above anything to be got by investing simply in securities or other financial obligations.

In its current operations a business will have a fluctuating need for finance. Certain rhythms make themselves felt: wages payments, weekly; salary payments, monthly; dividends, twice a year; taxes, at foreseeable points of time; payments for materials, again at more or less foreseeable points of time, with some latitude as to when the bills actually need be met.

On the other side of the account there will be payments coming in for goods supplied, and behind them the prospect of future payments to come for goods supplied on the understanding that they will be paid for later. The rhythm here gives rise to problems, because of the timing interval and the credit gap which has to be bridged. An increasing order-book may bring larger payments in time, but these may not be enough, given the need for extending credit, to make up for the larger and more immediate outgoings called for by increased production.

Taking both sides of the account, receipts and expenditure will not coincide; there will be a gap one way or another, and this gap will be fluctuating, partly in response to the rhythms already mentioned, partly under the impact of unforeseen changes. The gap will be reflected in the bank balance: the credits will grow or fall, or the debits met on overdraft decrease or rise.

One thing, for reasons already mentioned, the business will

try to avoid: the carrying of excess balances for an unnecessary period on its account. As long as those in charge can see opportunities for expanding the business and earning the higher rates of return which are expected from successful operation, they will have an inducement to tie up any spare resources in the business. (This inducement may be reinforced by special Government concessions given to encourage investment.) Idle balances at the bank—even if they are earning some interest on deposit—represent opportunities foregone. The smaller such balances, the more intensive is the use of the funds available.

This is one side of the picture. A business, however, is not only concerned with applying funds to its best long-term advantage, but it has to live with its bank. While a bank manager is content with accounts that turn over quickly, moving from debit to credit and back again, or even to some extent remaining in debit but financing a whole series of transactions in sequence, he will nevertheless hold the view that a successful business may be in need of fresh injections of permanent capital, and these he will not be prepared to provide. Nor will the business itself be content to remain at the mercy of its bank, so that it loses freedom of manœuvre if the unforeseen occurs. There are therefore limits to the extent to which bank finance can solve the problems of an undertaking, and these limits are important to the borrower as well as to the lender.

But not only must a business preserve some independence from its bank; it will be faced with situations where it may need deliberately to keep substantial balances at its disposal.

These will be funds which it is unable to put to work immediately in the business itself, but which are in excess of what can be usefully absorbed in the normal, day-to-day ebb and flow of outgoings and receipts. One can give examples of this. First, an undertaking with heavy equipment will be amortising it as time goes on, and the amounts set aside will accumulate. Some re-equipment is no doubt going on regularly, but there are bound to be irregular intervals between major programmes of re-equipment. Reserves which have to be built up for this purpose may therefore become substantial. The shipping industry is possibly the most spectacular example of this: fleets cannot be renewed in small pieces and major renewals will be unevenly spaced. Similar things can happen in any industry with large assets by way of equipment at its disposal which involve renewal in large lumps. In between spasms of re-equipment, substantial sums will have to be handled.

A second case is that of the business which at intervals has to raise new capital from outside because of the rate at which it is expanding. When it makes a new capital issue it will use the money in part to pay off loans from banks taken in anticipation of such refinancing, and in part it will carry a substantial margin in hand to take care of future phases of development expenditure. It is the latter portion, which for the time being must be left uncommitted, which presents problems of short-term investment.

A third case is rather different in character. It is that which is often described as arising from the 'speculative motive'. The business may be such that the ability to jump in with a large cash payment—whether to buy up another business, or to acquire property, or to pre-empt materials or finance an urgent contract—may be a major consideration. If one is to be poised to conduct such an operation, one does not want to have to negotiate a loan from a bank; quick and certain cash may be all-important to the success of the transaction. So in some types of business a liquid reserve for special manœuvres may be highly desirable.

Such illustrations show that successful undertakings may need to have within reach funds which they cannot use themselves for the moment: amortisation moneys, finance raised on new capital issues and as yet unspent, and amounts deliberately kept available to take up unforeseen opportunities at short notice. How are the resulting funds going to be held?

A company can always keep superfluous funds on deposit with its bank. This will be available at seven days' notice, but normally will earn only 2 per cent below bank rate. However, if it has connections with a bank other than a clearing bank, the rigid understandings do not apply, and it will probably get a better rate for large amounts.

If the company is a member of a group, there may be better short-term uses within the group. While a company dare not tie up such funds in its own business if it cannot realise them in a hurry, there may be opportunities of using them for temporary purposes within the group, the group thus being enabled to economise in its financing as a whole. The more economical use of funds is one of the advantages of large-scale organisations covering a range of companies.

Beyond this, there are two regular outlets. The most obvious for considerable amounts is that of investment in Treasury bills, which bring in only a little below bank rate, which run for three months, but which are easily realisable before maturity and which can often be acquired to mature on any particular date if it is known when the money will be needed. The minimum size of a Treasury bill is £5,000. In addition there may be other opportunities for investment in early-maturing Government securities.

The other major outlet is that of temporary deposits with local authorities. This has grown in importance over recent years. Such deposits command varying rates for varying periods: around bank rate for money on seven days' notice, and somewhat above for longer money. Such lending now presents a major opportunity for the employment of short-term funds.

One can add other forms of temporary financing which may meet the requirements of companies with funds to spare. Merchant bankers and money brokers may be able to arrange for the exploitation of such opportunities, and also to put lenders in touch with the local authority market or with finance houses in special need of funds.

The position of the business undertaking is therefore not unlike that of the private individual, except that at the liquid end the specialised alternatives offered to individuals in the shape of Government savings facilities are replaced for the company by Treasury bills and local authority loans, and other outlets working in fairly large sums. At the long end, a successful business will have its own requirements to meet, and will be setting aside money from its own earnings to enable it to expand.

4. The Banks and their Depositors

Banks are indebted to their customers for almost the whole of their resources.

Why is it that the public are content—as individuals and as proprietors of business undertakings—to see vast funds standing to their credit with the banks? Or to put the question more lightly: one can understand why bank managers are content to give overdrafts to their customers, since they will be collecting interest from their customers; but why should customers grant overdrafts to their banks—which is in effect what happens when an account is in credit—given that the banks pay modest interest only on the smaller part of these borrowings and no interest on the rest? In short, what are the inducements which make people content to hold bank balances on the scale they do?

The amounts involved are vast. In round figures, in the middle of May 1967 the London clearing banks owed on current account (payable on demand) some £5,000 million and on deposit (time) account over £3,500 million, making a total of £8,500 million. On current account the banks paid no interest; on the deposit account they were paying 3½ per cent, on which the recipients would have to pay tax. (The other side of the picture is that these banks had advanced to their customers some £5,000 million, £4,600 million by way of advances and the rest through the purchase of U.K. commercial bills.)

What has already been said about the handling of personal savings and business funds has thrown some light on this. The motives behind the willingness to hold current accounts (carrying no interest and involving bank charges) are essentially practical. They spare people having to hold physical cash, by giving them access to a means of making payment through a process of cancelling claims on specific instruction—that is, by writing cheques and in similar ways. The amount on current account may be large, but so is the volume of payments which have to be made. There is a moral in this for the banks: since they get the handling of these sums because of the facilities they give and not because of any return they offer, it is in their interest to keep these facilities as attractive as possible.

Amounts held on deposit are rather different: after all, one can still enjoy the payments and other facilities a bank has to offer if one puts temporarily superfluous funds elsewhere. Here on the face of it the banks seem even more vulnerable.

What then are the consequences of the banks' competing with each other—and also with other financial intermediaries— for depositors?

The consequences of competition between banks are much the same as competition in any other sphere. The bank which fails to satisfy its customers will lose accounts to its rivals; this will affect the whole of its organisation since it will be carrying that much less business; the overheads of banks are heavy; profits will be affected adversely; and so on. The bank will have to do better, or in the last resort let itself be absorbed by some more efficient bank.

But this is the less interesting part of the story. More to the point is the question: what happens to the banking system as such. After all, a cheque gets paid out of one bank account into another. Does that mean that the bank's customers are captives of the banking system as a whole?

To begin with, it is not quite exact to say that a cheque can only get paid from one bank account into another. It can be drawn out in cash. Or it can be paid to the Government. The Government does not keep its money with the commercial banking system but with the Bank of England. So the payment could leak out of the ordinary banking system, so to speak, except in so far as the Government uses the proceeds to pay off what it owes, as it usually does. Or the money can be paid away to someone outside the United Kingdom who repatriates it. (This comes to much the same thing, since the sequence could be a payment to a Government account—the Exchange Equalisation Account—which in its turn makes a payment for the benefit of the foreigner out of the exchange reserves.) But the question remains: leaving aside payments calling for cash, and payments for Government or foreign account, must we accept that since a cheque calls for payment from one banking account to another, the banking system is self-contained and cannot lose money, and so is immune from outside competition?

This is central. On the one hand, individuals quite clearly have a choice as to how much of their wealth they keep in liquid form in their bank accounts. On the other, the total volume of bank deposits appears, other things being equal (and disregarding cash and payments to the Government or foreigners), to be unalterable. How is this to be reconciled?

The answer is that the total volume of deposits (i.e. current and 'deposit' accounts together) can alter even if other things remain equal, i.e. the total flow of effective transactions to be financed, as well as the lending policy of the banks, remain the same. What happens is that a changed volume of deposits can revolve more or less rapidly and yet sustain an unchanged volume of business. Put in another way: a lender to a bank and a borrower from a bank can be brought together outside the bank, and, by doing business direct, can short-circuit the need for the bank loan.

Such an answer can be illustrated arithmetically. Before doing so, it is necessary to recall that banks in their relations with their customers are both borrowers and lenders. They pay their customers on their time deposits 2 per cent below bank rate. They charge their customers for the money they advance 1 per cent or 2 per cent above bank rate. The gap between borrowing and lending rates is therefore 3 to 4 per cent. What happens, then—to take a simplified illustration—if an intermediary with financial contacts finds he can narrow the margin, paying a little more than the banks do for the money he borrows and lending it for a shade less than the banks charge?

Assume such an intermediary, A.

The total deposits with the banks amount to £x.

A (the intermediary) borrows £1,000 from B, who has a credit balance with his bank.

Total deposits still remain at £x, but A, who has taken over the credit balances, owes B £1,000 outside the banking system.

A now lends the £1,000 to C, who is overdrawn by that amount at his bank.

C pays the £1,000 into his bank account. Instead of being in debit to the tune of £1,000, C's account with his bank is all square.

The banking system is owed £1,000 less by those borrowing from it, and owes £1,000 less to its depositors. The total volume of bank deposits is now £x minus £1,000.

Outside the banking system, C owes £1,000 to A, and A owes £1,000 to B.

The business which C was carrying on with his overdraft can continue as before; the bank has been entirely passive in the matter, with its lending policy unchanged; nevertheless the total volume of deposits is £1,000 less than it was before this sequence of transactions.

The bank, it is true, has it in its power to restore the position —that is, bring the total deposits back to £x—either (i) by lending £1,000 to someone to whom it had previously refused to lend; or (ii) by buying a security for £1,000 (in return for creating a deposit of the same amount) which otherwise it would not have bought. But this means a departure from the assumption of 'other things being equal'; the bank can only maintain the total volume of deposits by reversing a decision and making a loan or buying a security which otherwise it would not have done, and in the process opening up the possibility of a transaction by the recipient of the funds which previously he would not have been in a position to undertake.

Before leaving this narrow arithmetical demonstration, it is worth noticing that the process can operate conversely. If we assume that intermediaries which have been operating on the strength of a 3 to 4 per cent margin between bank lending and borrowing rates suddenly decide that the margin is too narrow, then borrowers will be thrown back on their banks in place of intermediaries, and will take up the loans they could have had but have refused because they could borrow more cheaply elsewhere. And the total of bank deposits will go up. In the terms of our example, C, having got into the habit of borrowing from A and finding this facility withdrawn, will borrow from his bank, and A will no longer want money from B, who will have his original deposit, and the total of deposits will be £1,000 higher than it would have been had the loan sequence outside the banks continued in operation.

The simplified proposition which has been set out points to significant consequences. It shows that the banks can be affected by outside competition *even though the outside competitors bank with them*. In the last resort the controlling factor is the *difference between* the rates at which the banks borrow and lend rather than the absolute height of either one of them. It is this difference which gives the competing intermediaries (such as non-clearing banks) scope for taking business away from banks (such as clearing banks).

In actual practice the transactions which take place are unlikely to follow the exact pattern set out above. When an intermediary has a use for funds and outbids a clearing bank for time deposits it will usually not find it necessary to undercut the bank in finding clients. Instead of charging less it is more likely that it will go further and charge more and relend the funds for some purpose which the bank is not prepared to support, either because of its own stricter lending standards or because the purpose is one which the authorities would wish discouraged. This will be especially so in times of credit restriction. In short, the intermediaries can use the funds which they have acquired more profitably in meeting the needs of excluded marginal borrowers and so eroding any restraints which the authorities may seek to impose. It is in this sense that outside lending most often flourishes in competition with the banks, thereby giving cause for complaint to the banks and problems for the authorities.

Nevertheless, it is important not to overlook the basic principle that it is theoretically possible for the intermediary both to outbid for deposits the clearing bank with which it holds an account and to relend the money so acquired at a cut rate in competition with the bank itself while adhering to the same standards as are applied by the bank. This holds good, even if in practice intermediaries succeed in discovering more remunerative outlets. In periods when credit is easy and borrowers hard to find, one might well see the intermediaries both outbidding and undercutting (to which the response of the banks would be to offer especially favourable arrangements to their more important clients).

This is inherent in an underlying situation where banks both borrow from their customers and to a large extent also lend to them. The customers who lend and borrow are separate entities, and if the banks pay too little (or give inadequate services) to those who lend to them, and charge too much to those who come to borrow from them, borrowers and lenders will have an inducement to come together and make their independent arrangements outside the commercial banking system. Intermediaries who can bring about these profitable introductions will do more business. Total deposits of banks will be lower than they would otherwise have been.

In the converse case, if the banks satisfy those who lend to them and in their turn lend on moderate terms to those who borrow from them, there will be the less scope for outside deals and for intermediaries, and the volume of bank deposits will remain higher.

In short, what it comes to is that banks are in competition not only between themselves but also with their own customers. What is more, this competition goes far beyond the terms of the narrow arithmetical example given. Intermediary A can borrow the £1,000 from B to lend at a higher rate of interest to somone unable to get a loan from a bank, or in circumstances where the bank has been instructed not to give loans of a particular character. A bank, after all, is borrowing its deposits from customers, and there is nothing to stop its customers lending their credit balances to anyone they choose. This has consequences when it comes to credit control. And for the banks the moral remains that they are subject to competitive influences not only between each other but as against their customers, and that in what they charge and the facilities they offer they are compelled to take account of this.

CHAPTER FOUR

Banks and Intermediaries as Lenders

1. *Banks and their Assets*

Banks are responsible for depositors' money, which they can be called on to repay forthwith or on very short notice.

This obligation is not as onerous as it seems. In the first place, no one would expect a leading bank (in this country) to be put in a position where it was unable to meet its obligations; in the event of a calamity, however caused, the Central Bank and Government would provide any support necessary. (In the United States, where the banking system is fragmented, there are Government-sponsored insurance facilities.) Second, people do not want to draw out cash for its own sake in order to hold it in large amounts in their own homes. Third, payments from an account in one clearing bank would for the most part normally turn up in another. The fear of a run on the banks has ceased to be a material factor in determining policy.

However, banks still have to make practical arrangements for meeting the demands upon them. Broadly—to take the London clearing banks—the disposition of assets is: one-third in liquid form, two-thirds in advances and investments.

The table opposite—based on figures published in the *Bank of England Quarterly Bulletin*—sets out the distribution of assets of the London clearing banks,

The items require explanation.

Items 1 to 3. This is the 'cash' base on which the banks operate. The 'till money'—notes and coin—held in the banks (item 1) can be supplemented by drawing further physical cash as required from the Bank, the balance (item 2) being debited or

London Clearing Banks: Distribution of Assets
(*As at 16 November 1966, with bank rate at 7 per cent. Figures in £ million.*
Percentages are those of gross deposits.)

1. Coin and notes		500	
2. Balances with Bank of England		278	
3. Total cash (1 + 2)		778	(8·3%)
4. Money to discount market	817		
5. Other money at call and short notice	328		
6. Total at call and short notice (4 + 5)		1,145	
7. Treasury bills	647		
8. Other U.K. bills	320		
9. Other bills	115		
10. Total bills discounted (7 + 8 + 9)		1,083	
11. *Total liquid assets* (3 + 6 + 10)		3,006	(31·9%)
12. *Special deposits with Bank of England*		189	
13. British Government stocks	1,022		
14. Other investments	141		
15. Total investments (13 + 14)		1,163	(12·3%)
16. Advances, etc.		4,562	(48·4%)
17. *Total investments and advances* (15 + 16)		5,725	(60·7%)
18. Total of assets (11 + 17), excluding special deposits		8,731	(92·6%)

credited in return for notes supplied or paid in. This balance also serves to settle net debits and credits, as thrown up in the clearing, between banks, or between a bank and the Bank of England itself. The split between notes and balances will partly depend on seasonal factors. Item 3 (the sum of 1 and 2) is by arrangement kept at a minimum of 8 per cent of gross deposits. If there is a shortage on item 2, the bank calls in money from the discount market (item 4 below) to replenish; if there is an excess, this is put into the market.

Items 4 to 6. This represents the second line of reserves. The discount market, which acts as a buffer between the Bank and the banks, borrows money for short periods—some overnight, much of the rest up to seven days—from the clearing banks and other institutional lenders, and invests it in the purchase of Treasury bills and short-dated Government bonds, as well as commercial bills, in all of which it deals. If hard pressed owing to a shortage of cash, it can go to the Bank of England, and borrow against them or rediscount them. (Bank rate is the minimum rate at which houses in the discount market can dispose of certain types of paper to the Bank, if need be.) The discount market is borrowing at a slightly lower rate than what it gets on the paper in which it invests; borrowing from the Bank will put up the average cost of its borrowed funds, so that it has an inducement to keep out of the Bank. But in the normal way the Bank is at pains to see that the market is supplied with adequate funds, and if the market is forced into the Bank it is as a matter of deliberate policy. Item 4 represents the total lent by the banks to the discount market. If a bank wants to increase its balance at the Bank, it will reduce the amount lent to the market, and conversely. Item 5 represents money at call and short notice lent elsewhere—miscellaneous items such as inter-bank loans and money on short loan to the stock market. Item 6 gives the total of the short loans which the banks can call in if they need to reinforce their cash position.

Items 7 to 10. These consist of bills—both Treasury and commercial—and the equivalent. They are obligations normally maturing within three months or less, and spread in such a way that a fair proportion comes in each day. Item 8 covers certain refinanceable export credits guaranteed by the E.C.G.D. Thus a bank can strengthen its cash position by not replacing bills as they are paid off. In addition, it could if pressed make arrangements with the help of the Bank of England to turn these assets into cash at short notice in case of need.

Item 11. This gives the total of liquid assets: cash (in tills and at the Bank); short loans; and bills. This is, as things stand at present, a key figure in the concept of credit control as exercised by the Bank of England. The figure shown in the table is equivalent to 31·9 per cent of the gross deposits of the banks. The basic understanding between the banks and the Bank of England is that the banks will maintain liquid assets at not less than 28 per cent of total deposits. As there is a seasonal movement in liquid assets, the banks aim at not less than 31 or 32 per cent towards the end of the year, to allow for the fall in the following quarter, the tax-paying season, when pressure is greatest.

To the extent that the Bank can influence directly the volume of liquid assets of the banks, it should in theory be able to influence indirectly the volume of advances plus investments. This follows from the arithmetical relationship, that if the banks lose a certain amount of liquid assets, they have to cut back investments and/or advances in addition by at least the equivalent of what they have lost. Thus if the Bank sells £100,000 of Government securities to the customer of a bank, both the balance of the customer with his bank, and the balance of the bank with the Bank of England, will be reduced by £100,000. But as the liquid assets of the bank sustain at least double that amount of other assets, if the proportion is to be maintained, the total of the less liquid assets must be reduced by over £200,000—the £100,000 which has already gone to pay for the securities, and a further £100,000 + to be achieved by the bank disposing of longer-term securities or by cutting down on advances. It is the gearing involved in the maintenance of this particular proportion that in theory provides the conventional basis of Bank of England control of bank credit.

In practice it is not as simple as this. The Bank's ability to influence the banks' liquid assets in this way has limitations which should be recognised. It cannot, for instance, sell securities unless someone wants to buy; that is to say it must pay attention to the need of maintaining the market in Government securities, and must therefore take account of its absorptive capacity. Moreover, the Bank's market operations cannot be divorced from the wider context of the Exchequer's financing requirements, in favour of the attempt to influence up or down, at will, the banks' liquidity position.[1]

Item 12. The conventional basis may not be enough. On this occasion the additional brake of special deposits is in operation. An amount equivalent to 2 per cent of total deposits has been segregated, and put aside with the Bank of England—who have re-lent it to the Government. Item 12 is intended as a reinforcement to the limit exercised on the basis of item 11. It is, as it were, a potentially liquid asset which has been disqualified from counting as such because the supply of liquidity was held to be excessive.

Items 13 to 15. These are the banks' investments—the longer-term securities held by the banks. They are less profitable than advances (see item 16 below) and have the disadvantage that when the rate of interest rises, while the return on advances goes up, the return on investments remains the same and their market value falls. (To compensate this, in the converse case there is a capital appreciation.) Much of the larger part (item 13) consists of British Government securities. At least half of them will mature within five years; the balance between five and ten. In a time of squeeze and rising interest rates, the banks can be faced with prospects of loss if they are forced to sell securities. Nevertheless they may need to sell in order to avoid having to press customers with overdrafts unduly, and differences of opinion can arise with the authorities as to how far they should do so.

Item 16. This is the main item: advances to customers, equivalent to over half the total deposits, and the most remunerative of all their assets. It is the banks' lending policy in this respect that can stimulate or retard effective demand in the economy; it is here that the banks must seek their main earnings; it is the policy in respect of credit creation through the

---

[1] Some critics have, however, argued that traditional methods of control have been abandoned too easily; see below, pp. 102–4.

granting or withholding of advances that is central to monetary arrangements.

Items 17 and 18. These give the totals of 'non-liquid' assets, if they may be so described, under 17, and of all assets—apart from the special deposits—under 18. At the same date the corresponding figures for deposits were £9,421 million gross and £8,689 million net, the difference between the two being accounted for by balances with, and cheques in course of collection on, other banks in the United Kingdom, and items in transit between offices of the same bank. The percentages in the table are calculated on the gross deposits, and come to 92·6 per cent of the total, or something under 95 per cent if the disregarded special deposits are included. The assets exceed the net deposits, once the double-counting has been eliminated, with the special deposits included.

One may conclude by reverting to a paradox. The balances of the clearing banks with the Bank of England are an asset of the clearing banks and a liability of the Bank of England. Yet the Bank ultimately would exercise control over the banks—were it in a position to revert to conventional practice—by threatening to meet its liabilities. This threat is not that of sending round notes with which to pay off the banks' deposits, but that of selling some of its holdings of securities to the banks' customers. If this happens, the customer will hold Government debt in place of a deposit. The bank will see its liability reduced to the customer by an equivalent amount. But to complete the circle the bank will have lost an equivalent asset in the form of a reduction in its balance with the Bank, and the consequent fall in liquidity will compel it to make further reductions in its advances.

2. *The Cumulative Creation of Credit*

A purchaser of goods—whether of a motor-car or a parcel of groceries—who arranges to pay later, receives credit. The seller who has given credit has to think about replacing the goods, and taking credit from the wholesaler in his turn. The necessity of maintaining the flow of goods puts some limit on the amount of credit which can be given, and the point at which this will operate will depend on the bank balances of sellers and wholesalers and the possibility of adding to them by borrowing.

The obligations with which a bank is concerned do not directly involve goods. A bank is a dealer in financial obligations. When someone borrows from a bank, all he acquires in the first instance is liquidity, in the form of a right to make a payment in return for repayment at a later date plus interest. The bank has to watch, not the replacement of goods, but the flow of future repayments. Creating credit is for a bank a matter of providing liquidity. What are the limits to how far this process by which the banks create credit (i.e. provide liquid balances which can be used to make payments) can go?

To begin with the Bank of England. When the Bank pays for a security it has bought, it credits the account of the bank concerned on its books. The bank's balance with the Bank will be increased by a given amount. If the purchase is from a member of the public, the bank will have credited its customer with the same amount. If the purchase is direct from a bank, there may in the first instance be a switch from investments into (liquid) deposits with the Bank. In either case the bank will be in a position to make a further loan to its customers, while still maintaining the ratio of liquid assets to deposits.

Is there any limit on the Bank of England to restrict the amount of securities it can acquire, thereby swelling the balances of the clearing banks with it? If it increases the balance of one clearing bank, payments go to the accounts of other clearing banks, so that the sums in question go round and round in the Bank of England books and cannot escape (if we ignore any demand for notes and coin and for payment overseas) from the total of deposits in the Bank's books. In theory the limit on what it does is imposed by the Bank's own decisions. It is these decisions, taken after considering the consequences which would flow for the economy, which would determine the balances to be left to the credit of the clearing banks in total. In practice, however, these decisions are bound to be dominated by the need to make provision for the requirements of the Exchequer, so that the decisions of the monetary authorities are likely to be the outcome of conflicting motives.

The corresponding process by which the clearing banks create deposits in favour of the public is the same in character but slightly different in practice. Within the limits of the liquidity ratio, a clearing bank can create a deposit in favour of a customer by buying a security from him or by making him a loan. When he spends his money he will be paying into someone else's account. If the recipient has his account with the same bank, that bank's liquid assets are unchanged. If the recipient banks with another clearing bank, there has to be settlement by a corresponding payment between the banks, which will affect their accounts at the Bank of England, the account of the paying bank going down and that of the receiving bank going up. The effect of this—having regard to the liquidity ratio—is that the receiving bank has room for expansion and the buying bank should contract. However, this process will be going on all the time in both directions, and the outcome is that the clearing banks together can go on creating credit as long as they apply much the same standards, but if one bank goes ahead lending more freely than its fellows it will tend to lose out on its inter-bank balance of payments, having to pay more to the other banks at the expense of its reserves. Liquidity considerations will force the bank losing reserves to be more restrictive in its lending, while the receiving banks will be in a position to expand. In the converse case a bank which lent more slowly would gain on its reserves. Within the liquid-asset conventions, the banks as a whole can go a long way in expanding credit, as long as they keep in line.

But are there any limits beyond that? There may be a pressure on the liquid assets of the banks. We have already seen—in the context of the bankers and their depositors—that there are certain limitations. First, the Bank of England may intervene and sell securities. These will be paid for ultimately out of the accounts of the banks with the Bank, and to that extent the banks will see reserves extinguished. In the second place, the accounts of the Government sector are kept with the Bank of England and not with the banks. So that if the banks are called on for any reason to make payments to the Government sector, their reserves will again be depleted. (However, the converse case of large Government outlays increasing the banks' liquid assets have the opposite effect of increasing the banks' reserves.) Third, there are a set of payments which also would go to Government account because the Exchange Equalisation Account is the repository of our foreign exchange reserves. In so far as the banks' expansion of credit led to increased expenditure abroad, the demand for foreign exchange would be reflected in payments from the clearing bank reserves to the exchange authorities, a part of the Government sector, and the banks' balances with the Bank correspondingly reduced.

The analysis so far has been conducted on the assumption that—within accepted limits—the banks can increase deposits if they think fit. In fact, will they? Will they always be able to find securities which they want to buy, or borrowers to whom they would be willing to lend?

It cannot be assumed that there is always a queue of unsatisfied borrowers waiting to borrow money from their bank managers. That is the position during a period of credit stringency. But once the squeeze is over, there comes a phase when bank managers are again looking for customers who will take money for the sort of purposes for which banks like lending. The demand for bank credit may not be there. Or it may be there potentially, but being met by financial intermediaries competing with the banks.[1]

It is well to recollect that banks are not only competing

---

[1] This is the other leg of the process described on pp. 63–6. The intermediaries compete with the banks in borrowing, as described there, and also in lending, as here.

amongst themselves, but also against their own customers. A customer with a large existing balance on his account at his bank may be on the lookout for suitable opportunities to invest it. The borrower has a choice: he can either go to the bank and borrow from it, or he can go and find someone else with a large credit balance at the bank and borrow that balance from him. In practice there are intermediary institutions which help to do this. In the first case, the bank has increased its earning assets and its deposits. In the second case the deposits remain unchanged, but the need is met because an existing deposit has been made available to the borrower and is circulating more rapidly.

Nor is this competition between banks and outside lenders confined to periods of easy money. One of the complaints of the clearing banks is that during a period of restriction, when they are debarred from lending because of official policy, outside lenders come in and meet the needs of those turned down at a high rate of interest and at profit to themselves. These outside competitors are financial institutions who make their bank balances available to others.

The fact is that non-clearing banks and other intermediary institutions, with an account with a clearing bank and not with the Bank of England, can in their turn—within limits—create credit and so inject liquidity on the basis of their own bank balances. The volume of deposits or of advances made by the banks themselves is not alone a sufficient limiting factor. When one comes to consider methods of control, it will become apparent that to control only the clearing banks may not be enough, and controls may have to go much further if excess liquidity in the system is to be avoided.

It must be recognised that to rely on conventions based on the proportion of liquid assets at the disposal of the banking system is not by itself a sufficient basis of control. Even when it can be used effectively to control the clearing banks, there remains this problem of the activities of the intermediary institutions who do not hold their reserve balances with the Bank of England. In addition there is the further problem of meeting the authorities' own need for finance, not only for current outlays but for capital transactions.

3. *The Banks, the Bank of England and the Discount Market*

When the banks want to increase the amount standing to their credit at the Bank of England, they normally do it by a triangular transaction: they recall money lent to the discount market, and this repayment swells their balance at the Bank. As we have seen, the discount market is a feature peculiar to Britain; in other countries banks would in the usual way rediscount appropriate short-term paper direct with the central bank.

The discount market is best regarded as a market in the conventional sense. The members of the London Discount Market Association—a dozen houses—are dealers in a limited range of short-term securities. Their stock-in-trade consists of a pool of such securities which they finance by borrowing spare funds for short periods. They can do this on a large scale, even though their own capital is small, because they know that the Bank of England will give them support, and in case of necessity they can as of right resell to it (rediscount) certain categories of these short-term securities on their own initiative.

The structure of the market can best be shown by setting out the assets and liabilities of the institutions of which it is composed (see table opposite).

There were also borrowings of £5 million from the Bank of England outstanding at that date.

The existence of a money market such as this arises from the demand by banks and other institutions for a constant supply of short-term securities with a spread of maturity dates to fit in with particular requirements to enable them to use their assets to the best advantage. The banks by convention buy their Treasury bills through a discount house as opposed to tendering direct for Treasury bills at the weekly tender. Other institutions will have requirements which a particular assortment of bills from a discount house can meet.

Assets and Liabilities of Discount Market
(As at end of September 1966. Figures in £ million.)

Assets

British Government stocks	456
Treasury bills	333
Commercial bills, etc.	358
Other assets	155
Total	1,302

(*Note:* The Government stocks would mainly be maturing in two years, and almost all within five years.)

Liabilities

Their holdings were largely financed by borrowings from

Clearing banks	822
Scottish banks	78
Other domestic banks	22
Accepting houses and overseas banks	193
Other sources	98
Total	1,213

A market in short-term investments—largely Treasury bills, short-dated Government bonds and commercial bills—explains itself: it maintains a supply of and provides short-term investment bonds of varying maturities to meet particular needs. What requires more explanation is why it should be operated on the basis of a large volume of funds lent at very short notice and always subject to recall, frequently exercised, and made possible by a safety-valve procedure. The answer is that the market does meet one need in particular. If on the day's operations one bank —say the Midland—has paid out much more than it gets in, it will recall money from the market. But by definition the money which the Midland has paid has been received by other banks; and the market is likely to be able to borrow from the receiving banks what it has to pay the Midland. The clearing banks in the first instance settle with each other through their accounts at the Bank of England. At a level once removed further adjustments take place through a change in the ownership of the funds advanced at call and short notice to the market.

The market—as has already been noted—is the regular source of supply of Treasury bills to the banks. It has a further function, that of facilitating the process of placing Treasury bills when they are issued each week. This is a central feature of the day-to-day management of the money market as at present practised. The Bank of England, on behalf of the Treasury, operates an auction: a given amount of Treasury bills is on offer, and institutions tender for them. Those that offer the highest price (i.e. demand the least discount for tying up funds for three months) get what they ask for as long as their bid is not below that of the market. The market collectively will put in a uniform bid sufficient to 'cover the tender', and so will underwrite the offer. This means that all the outside bidders who offer the more favourable terms get their allocations in full; the market takes up the balance. This procedure, by which the offer is underwritten by what looks like a dealers' ring, serves the purposes of the Bank and the Treasury: dealers, auctioneer and customers are all—as it were—in collusion. The Treasury bills get placed and needs are met, and the Government gets it money.

The relationship between the Bank and the market is thus a complex one. On the one hand, it can be regarded as a business relationship, a piece of bargaining about some short-term securities which one party wishes to dispose of and the other to acquire to hold and resell in the course of a business which it is conducting for profit. On the other, it is also an association in the common task of renewing and distributing a certain portion of the Government debt. This double relationship is shown in the treatment which the Bank gives to the discount houses. At one time the Bank will give help and support to the market when it is short of funds, taking the initiative in buying bills at current rates. At another, when there is a difference of opinion

between the Bank and the market, the market may be forced
into the Bank to borrow at penal rates; relief will then be forthcoming only at a rate which puts up the average cost of the
market's borrowed funds. The Bank is thus at the same time
concerned to see that the market is in a position to carry on
business in such a way that the tender is taken up, but also to
control it so that it does not make credit too cheap when, for
example, a movement against sterling makes a tightening-up
desirable.

The peculiar structure which keeps in being a money market
of a kind which does not exist in any other country is defended
on the ground that the system works and is reasonably cheap to
run. But the explanation of its survival goes rather deeper than
this. The market exists in its present form because it makes easy
certain bargaining relationships, maintains a balance between
the several parties, and to some extent preserves confidentiality.
If the normal reinforcement of funds came by the banks redis-
counting straight with the Bank, the banks could feel embarrassment at explaining their needs; the automatic relationship—not
calling for explanation—would not be easy to maintain. But
when a bank calls in money from the market, there is no question of explanation; and if the market in its turn has to borrow
from the Bank, the explanation is simply that it is short of cash,
and why those who normally lend to it are calling in the money
is not something for which it can be held responsible. So the
existence of a discount market is said to help to maintain peace
and stability, and to do so at a reasonable price. However, to
set out the reasons is not to defend the arrangement, which
could be open to criticism as an anachronism in a world where
the closest working between the several monetary authorities is
so obviously desirable.

When the Bank of England does wish to intervene, it normally
does so in the discount market through its bill-broker (the so-
called 'Special Buyer') and in the gilt-edged market on the
Stock Exchange through the Government Broker. But this may
not be enough for the purposes of the day-to-day monetary

management. In particular the Bank on occasion finds it convenient to buy Treasury bills from the banks themselves (which it does through its bill-broker) so that the banks are in funds and have an inducement to increase their lending to the discount market and to buy Treasury bills from it for themselves. This is the so-called 'indirect' help to the discount market; the 'direct' help is that given when the purchases are directly from the market. Such is the process by which the market is enabled to take up and handle the volume of Treasury bills coming forward each week. If it is a question of cutting back, the authorities have to look outside the discount market and resort to such reinforcements to monetary management as special deposits. In order to curtail liquidity the London clearing and Scottish banks are required to set aside out of their balances at the Bank of England an amount equivalent to a given proportion of the gross deposits—towards the end of 1966 some £200 million, representing(in the case of the London banks) 2 per cent of deposits with them. As we saw, the special deposits are shown as a separate item and—though they earn approximately the same as Treasury bills—they are sterilised in the sense that they are disregarded for the purpose of calculating liquid assets.

Had this £200 million been freely available to the clearing banks and conformed to the current pattern, it would have gone to reinforce the liquid assets of the banks; some £60 million as cash and balance with the Bank of England, and the rest as money at call and short notice and Treasury and other bills. On this foundation, again assuming the current pattern, the banks could have increased advances by £300 million and added another £100 million to their investments. They have every inducement to do so: it would make them better off to the tune of £20 million a year.[1]

[1] The arithmetic (taking bank rate at 7 per cent and Government stocks around a 7 per cent basis) is as follows (figures in £ million). Gross receipts for added advances, 24 (assuming only 1 per cent above bank rate); gross receipts from added investments, 7; total gross receipts, 31. Deduct 5 to allow for the fact that special deposits earn interest while the portion of liquid assets held as cash and balances at the Bank does not. Deduct 7½ to

The use of special deposits is a reminder of how the discount market has lost in importance as a controlling mechanism: not only has the Bank of England to help it by acquiring from time to time Treasury bills straight (by the indirect method) from the banks but when it is time to put the brakes on seriously the Bank has to go straight ('indirectly' seems even more inappropriate here) to the banks and impound the requisite proportion of their reserves.

But the discount market has also lost in relative importance as a money market. A recent survey[1] of what has been happening in the London short-term money markets lists them with the order of magnitude of the resources at their disposal at the end of 1965:

	(£ million)
Discount houses	1,400 (total resources)
Finance houses	600 (deposits)
Local authorities	1,700 (temporary borrowing)
Euro-dollars	2,000
Inter-bank market	1,000

The discount market, the established market, is being pushed aside by the newcomers. Of these, the Euro-dollar market will be discussed at length in due course. The last—the inter-bank market—relates to the non-clearing banks: those banks, largely with overseas connections, who keep their reserve balances not with the Bank of England but with the clearing banks themselves. The funds at the disposal of this market are used to maintain the necessary liquid balances to settle transactions between each other from day to day. It is here we see the customers of the clearing banks lending to each other outside

allow for that part of the 400 deposits created which will receive interest (2 per cent below bank rate) as opposed to interest-free current accounts. Total deductions, 12½. Net receipts 18½, and possibly more as the rate assumed for advances is on the low side.

[1] 'London's "New" Markets for Money', *Midland Bank Review* (August 1966). The actual figures of local authority temporary debt at the end of 1965 are given in the *C.S.O. Financial Statistics* for June 1966 as: up to seven days (in £ million) 1,257; over seven days, up to three months, 307; over three months, up to twelve months, 234. Total, 1,798.

the clearing banks themselves, in order to enable each to keep its balance at the clearing bank at what it regards as an appropriate level. The funds are dealt in—we are told—in large round amounts and may include Euro-dollars swapped into sterling.

So again we come up against the problem of exercising control in respect of lending between intermediaries all at one remove from the Bank of England, since the clearing banks come in between.

4. *Liquidity and the Indebtedness of the Public Sector*

The financial structure has public debt built into every side and every corner—the outcome of two world wars. The times when it came into being were those of shortage, control and rationing; had there not been these constraints, the resulting repercussions could have destroyed the price structure and in due course the debt itself. But there was no collapse; the debt has been absorbed.

One must expect public debt to go on increasing. On current account the Central Government should be reducing the debt, taking one year with another, assuming no wars or catastrophes, and assuming also that the need for maintaining effective demand does not make a deliberate policy of deficit financing appropriate. But an increase in debt will be made necessary by new investment in the public sector. The building of houses by public authorities, more power stations to meet the rising electricity load, new and improved communications, schools and hospitals, all call for investment which will bring in returns either directly in money terms or indirectly to the community, but which must in the first instance be paid for out of borrowings. These may be in the form of direct obligations of the Central Government itself (some of the sums involved being re-lent to the authorities concerned) or may be direct liabilities of these authorities: for example, direct borrowings of local authorities from private sources, or borrowings of nationalised industries from the banks.

Two other kinds of borrowing—specialised in character—should also be noted. A surplus on international account gives occasion for an increase in Government borrowing, and a deficit for a reduction. In simplified terms, what happens is that if a favourable balance of payments leads to the U.K. receiving foreign currency or gold, this has to be bought by the authorities for sterling. The authorities will raise sterling on Treasury bills, the counterpart being the gold or foreign exchange added to the reserves. Treasury bills outstanding will be increased; reserves will be increased by a corresponding amount. (The actual process would be that as a result of trade or capital movements, foreign currencies would be offered to the authorities. They would pay for these currencies in sterling, raised against additional borrowing. They could then either hold these currencies; or use them to pay off outstanding obligations in foreign currencies; or turn them into gold to add to the reserves.) Whatever the exact form the series of transactions takes, the outcome of a favourable balance on international account is an increase in Government borrowing balanced by an improvement in the reserve position of the authorities vis-à-vis overseas countries.

In the converse case, a deficit on international account will lead to a fall in the reserves accompanied by a fall in Government borrowing. To illustrate: traders have to pay out more in foreign currencies than they get in. They go to the authorities to acquire the necessary foreign exchange. They pay sterling to the authorities for the dollars, francs or marks which they need. These sterling receipts lead to the authorities reducing their debts, the volume of Treasury bills outstanding being reduced. But of course the authorities have to find the foreign currency, and their gold and currency reserves are correspondingly reduced.

A British spectator of economic events should therefore in present circumstances be cheered by an *increase* in Government debt (largely Treasury bills) arising from a strong balance of payments leading to increased gold and foreign exchange reserves, and correspondingly downcast by a *reduction* in Government debt arising from a run on the pound which brings down our reserves. The point needs making at this length, because of the instinctive feeling that an increase in debt is a bad thing and a reduction a good one. Here the converse is the case. One can reflect that successful businesses expand on increasing debt, even though failing businesses may also find their debts increasing.

Another form of indebtedness of concern to the authorities is that of Government-supported export credit. The volume of credit extended to foreigners buying our goods is growing. The sums due in the future from overseas buyers are assets of the United Kingdom, and over time as they are paid they support our balance of payments. But in the meantime the exporters are unpaid, and have to be financed. Government-sponsored guarantees ensure that in the interval they can get their money from the banks. These are not Government borrowings (the Government will only have to pay where buyers fail to pay, and this is met from insurance premiums paid by exporters), but as exports are in the vital national interest, it is concerned in seeing that these export finance facilities are maintained and used. It follows that, in making arrangements for the effective handling of public sector debt, the authorities have also to leave full scope for the demand for export finance.

To sum up: one would expect the borrowings of the public sector to increase from year to year, if only because of the investment for which the Government, local authorities, nationalised industries and other public bodies are responsible between them. Further, there may have to be increasing borrowings to finance increased holdings of gold and foreign exchange reserves. In addition, there is a public interest in seeing that the financial system adequately covers the requirements of the export trade in so far as it can be expected to give credit to its foreign buyers.

The authorities have to fit these increased borrowings into the financial structure. They face two conflicting forces. On the one hand the debt must be placed in such a way that it does not give rise to excessive liquidity, as it would if it were largely placed with the banks on the basis of increased reserves made available by the Bank of England. On the other hand, the cost of the debt has to be met, and everyone wants to keep this cost as low as possible.

These conflicting forces restrict the freedom of manœuvre of the authorities. To the extent that debt is placed with the banks, it can be the basis for further expansion in the private sector because of the added liquidity. But the cost of borrowing will be less. On the other hand, to the extent that it is placed on terms attractive to purchasers outside the banking system, the cost to the community is likely to be greater. But the danger of expansion is avoided since those who take up the long-term debt lose liquidity, and the banking system is not in a position to reinstate it by increased lending. The need to control the credit position and the need to keep down the cost of borrowing have to be balanced against each other.

Borrowing cheaply usually means borrowing on short-term. In the hands of the banks, additions to short-term Government debt mean additions to lending power. In the hands of the public, additions to short-term Government debt (unless it is of a type likely to be firmly held) can mean an addition to potential spending power and also give rise to problems of refinancing. A large volume of outstanding Treasury bills means that it is always open to holders to let them run off, and use the proceeds for increased spending, for example, if they expect prices to rise. In the same way a large volume of outstanding short-term borrowings by local authorities—over £1,250 million recallable on seven days' notice—leaves the authorities in an exposed position since if they try to restrict credit, such short-term loans from domestic sources may not be renewed, and the local authorities' refinancing has still to be taken care of.

So far the problem has been envisaged in terms of prospective additions to public-sector debt. This is the realistic assumption, since we must expect public-sector borrowing to keep pace with the private sector as national income increases. Indeed it would not be unexpected if public investment required an increasing proportion of the resources available year by year.

However, it is perhaps excessive to assume that public-sector borrowing (widely defined) must increase every year without interruption, and the consequences of debt reduction deserve some passing attention. Assume (perhaps a remote contingency) that a cut in military commitments makes possible net reductions in outstanding debts and that Government obligations are being extracted from the financial structure in which they are embedded. What happens?

A sudden reduction would cause dislocation. How far it would do so would depend on whether it was foreseen and what action the authorities took to minimise any disruption. They could, for example, buy in long-term bonds—i.e. unfund—to the extent needed to maintain the liquidity of the banking system. A large temporary reduction should be manageable as long as it is foreseen.

Carrying imagination further, and assuming a gradual reduction to the public debt over a period of years, there are a number of consequences to be noted. In the first place, authorities would gain in their ability to control the monetary system, since they would have room for manœuvre in the handling of the structure of the debt and their capacity to fund or unfund in the process: that is, they can choose how far they make reductions at the short-term (Treasury bill) end or at the long-term (gilt-edged) end. Second, the banking system would have every inducement to differentiate in the form taken in respect of lending to non-Government borrowers so as to throw up the maximum of commercial bills or other self-liquidating paper which might qualify as liquid assets in place of Government paper withdrawn. Third, a point would come where the conventions governing the liquidity ratio may have to be renegotiated.

Having said this, it must be confessed that there is a more

important consideration which so far has been omitted. The authorities cannot just be concerned with withdrawing debt. We must assume that they have been more preoccupied with taking steps to maintain the flow of effective demand. It will be their policy to stimulate growth in so far as stimulus (which presumably costs money) may be necessary. So the assumption of debt reduction is not only inherently unlikely, but may prove unworkable because the economic situation calls for lower taxes and/or increased expenditure leading to a deficit. In short, the need to keep the economy expanding may make hay of the assumption that the Government can go on reducing its debt.

But certain more concrete matters do emerge from this discussion. Thus it is clear that while sudden changes would cause some dislocation, it is not impossible for the system to adapt itself to gradual changes and still maintain appropriate conditions of liquidity. Second, the past injections of large volumes of public debt into the system took place under conditions of war when supplies were rationed and the lack of things on which to spend money made a build-up of liquid assets fairly harmless. Third, a similar build-up over a relatively short period in conditions of powerful economic activity would be bound to have an overwhelming effect on prices, in the absence of increased resources. (There are countries where we can see this at work even now.) Fourth, a massive reduction in the public-sector debt could only be undertaken successfully in conditions where in theory a great expansion in the private sector compensates for the reduction of spending in the public sector. This would be unlikely in practice at a time when the surpluses of the public sector which are paying off the debt are limiting consumption demand. What would be more probable would be that the Government would have to take steps by reducing taxes to leave people with more to spend. And reducing taxes is not consistent with reducing Government debt.

5. *Other Banks and Financial Institutions*

So far the analysis has been directed to the central features of the system—the clearing banks, the discount market and the Bank of England—against the background of a substantial volume of borrowings for public purposes. It remains to say something about the other banks (i.e. banks other than those of the London clearing) and the financial institutions.

The former include the Scottish and Northern Ireland banks; the larger merchant banks (which come under the heading of accepting houses in the Bank of England statistics) and the overseas banks of several kinds. The financial institutions cover building societies and hire-purchase finance companies; the Special Investment Departments of the Trustee Savings Banks; unit trusts and investment trusts; and the insurance companies and pension funds.

With the insurance companies and pension funds, there are no problems of sudden withdrawal. The money comes in steadily in an increasing flow. The calculations of the actuary make known in advance the amounts needed to meet the policies as and when they mature. The main task is to get the constant flow of money profitably invested over a wide spread of medium-term and long-term assets. These institutions have a great part in providing investment funds both for the public and private sector, but their task, however important, is a relatively placid one.

Investment trusts also are unlikely to be faced by liquidity problems. On the other hand, unit trusts, which really are investment trusts with what they offer done up in convenient packages to appeal to the general public, do have such a problem. These units enjoy a guarantee that they can be cashed on the basis of the market value of the underlying securities, and a figure is announced daily at which the managers of the trust will buy in unit-trust certificates. The managers of the trust therefore have the problem of covering themselves in the market.

The Investment Departments of the Trustee Savings Banks

are investing mainly in Government and local authority borrowings, and their concern is not so much that of finding enough short-term liquid assets as of getting a yield overall sufficient to satisfy their depositors.

With the building societies and the hire-purchase finance houses we are nearer to the banking field, since the managers of such institutions have to watch both what is coming in and also what is going out, since either might prove volatile. The building societies have special tax arrangements, and are in a position to pay their 'shareholders' or 'depositors' free of income tax (though not surtax). On the other hand, people who borrow from building societies to buy houses are relieved of tax in respect of the interest element on the loan while they are not assessed for income tax on the annual value of the houses they occupy themselves. All these concessions give strength to the movement.

The only special advantage enjoyed by the hire-purchase finance houses is that the business which they cover brings in a very high return: up to 20 per cent or more per annum is the real interest charge to the ultimate purchaser under a hire-purchase transaction. This leaves room for the finance houses to borrow the money they want by offering rates of interest which make the business attractive to many lenders and still leave ample room for costs, commissions, profits and risks. The rates at which the larger established houses take in money vary a good deal, but $7\frac{1}{2}$ or 8 per cent would be on the high side, and there is a long way to go from this to the figure of something between 15 and 20 per cent. The margin is wide enough to take care of costs and risks. Of course, the risks are there: the stronger purchasers will graduate to bank accounts and overdrafts on which tax paid can be deducted, so that hire-purchase facilities are left for the less credit-worthy. But the margins are such that the money can usually be found. This contrasts with the building societies where the inflow of money is variable by way of reaction to bank rate changes, while the rates offered to lenders and charged to borrowers are kept stable within limits.

One must return to the 'other' banks—those outside the London clearing. They fall into three groups, and have this in common: though they may have accounts with the Bank of England, they do not carry working balances on these accounts. Their liquid balances would be with the clearing banks.

The first of these groups—the Scottish and Northern Ireland banks—carry on straightforward banking business in their parts of the British Isles. The service provided is broadly similar to that given in England by the ordinary banking system, but there are differences: for example, a number of these banks issue notes of their own, all of which over and above an 'authorised' portion are covered by Bank of England notes and coin. The Scottish banks have been called on to put up special deposits with the Bank of England, but at a smaller proportion to total deposits than the London clearing banks.

The other two groups are more specialised in character: they are the large merchant banks (the accepting houses) and the several classes of banks operating overseas. Much of the accepting houses' business is connected with overseas transactions also.

A broad indication of the relative size of the various types of banks is given by their respective deposits. The net deposits of the domestic banks (the London clearing banks, plus the Scottish and Northern Ireland banks) would be some £10,000 million (the Scots and Northern Irish being responsible for over £1,000 million of this). Against this the accepting houses have deposits of something over £1,000 million and the overseas banks well over £4,000 million—an overall total of more than £15,000 million.

We have already described the accepting houses: independent banks, private in origin though now largely public in form, with a commercial rather than an industrial bias. In origin many of them are associated with family fortunes, as the names recall: Rothschilds, Hambros, Barings, Lazards, Warburgs. They are engaged in finding remunerative outlets for their own and related money and that managed by them for friends and associates. They have at their disposal special information and experience; they have widespread connections and knowledge of those with whom they are dealing; they can arrange temporary finance, or they can get a new issue on the market underwritten by means of the underwriting lists they have built up. Their outlook is largely directed overseas. Until recently the influence of these family banks in the City was very considerable, and although losing some ground and having to face amalgamations, they are still in a powerful position.

The overseas banks are a formidable reminder of the worldwide ramifications of sterling.

The following table sets out certain selected features.

Accepting Houses and Overseas Banks in the United Kingdom
(*Figures relate to September 1966*)

	Current and Deposit Accounts (£ million)		Loans to U.K. Local Authorities	Advances to Overseas Residents
	Total	Of which residents overseas		
Accepting houses	1,105	405	215	256
British overseas and Commonwealth banks	1,726	1,092	148	485
American banks	2,049	1,479	30	1,399
Foreign banks and affiliates	474	309	45	114
Other overseas banks	971	539	91	463
	6,325	3,824	528	2,716

Of the current and deposit accounts of residents overseas, £2,610 million represented currencies other than sterling—though this includes the currencies of overseas Sterling Area countries. The corresponding figure for advances was £2,457. The American banks' advances to overseas residents would be overwhelmingly Euro-dollar advances. The volume of short-term loans to U.K. local authorities is noteworthy.

The large amounts involved would be a sign of strength and source of profit if sterling were strong and the U.K. balance of payments continuously favourable. But there are difficulties in operating an international reserve currency when reserves are low and there is a continuing deficit on international account. The operations of the overseas banks and the accepting houses, as well as the short-term financing of the local authorities, are matters which will be examined further.

CHAPTER FIVE

The Mechanics of Control

1. *The Scope of Financial Control*

Changes in the rate of acquisition of goods and services directly affect production, employment, prices and the balance of payments. Control of the economy operates through regulating the scale of effective demand. Demand is determined in a large measure by Government: by what the tax-gatherer allows to the community in the way of spending power; by the outlays of the public sector; by the inducements given to enterprise to invest and expand.

The technical handling of the financial machine is only one of several forces which can exert an influence on demand, though in certain circumstances it can become dominant. In particular, when action is needed to restrain or stimulate demand, financial aspects need to be so handled as to avoid overstimulating expansion or adding an excessive restrictive influence.

Financial control works by influencing liquidity. Liquidity represents capacity for *settling* obligations, and in the context of rational decisions this comes to the same thing as capacity for *entering into* obligations. It is through decisions on prospective spending that effective demand is determined.

Liquidity by itself is not the major determinant of expenditure. For this one would look to income. Spending is a repetitive process, and in the ordinary way it is the flow of income that maintains the flow of demand. But there are always variations, and at critical moments other factors gain in importance. Where, for example, there is a general feeling that prices of goods are going to rise, the real determinant can become the size of existing possessions as much as income. To the extent that holders of assets can borrow on them or dispose of them without loss they can increase their outlay on goods in the expectation of a gain in money terms once prices have risen. The very fact that prices have risen—which means that the value of physical assets has risen—increases their capacity to enter into obligations. Inability to borrow on satisfactory terms, or the necessity of disposing of assets at a loss, can put a restraint on the increase in spending; but if a large volume of outstanding assets is widely diffused and in liquid form—such as short-term debt which can be cashed without loss or difficulty—the means of payment are at hand and there is nothing to stop spending racing ahead of income. It is in such a situation that excess liquidity becomes a danger. This is the reason why there is a financing problem for public authorities, and why they cannot just go ahead issuing a large volume of short-term obligations.

It is against such a background that we have to look at the actual technical means of controlling spending power. Leaving aside how far the flow of income may be increased or decreased through changes in the size of budgetary surpluses or deficits, the possible repercussions of a given flow of spending can still be influenced. The example of the structure of public-sector borrowing—the distribution of differing maturities—is one field in which there is room for manœuvre. A related field is that of the ease with which banks are prepared to supply finance; here there is scope for a variety of controls imposed on the banking system.

Controls can be of different types, and are to be looked at from different angles.

In the first place, there is a distinction between two broad classes. There are general controls which apply over the whole field of credit irrespective of the use to which money may be put. Side by side with these there are discriminating controls which affect particular types of activity: these include both discrimination in lending policy and special conditions attaching to particular kinds of business.

Second, there is a difference in method. On the one hand there is control exercised through the amount of finance made available at a given price. On the other, there is control by price: you can have as much money as before, but you must pay more for it. The distinction here is between access to money and cost of money. The two are not entirely separate, since it is usually possible, when the amount of credit available to a given borrower is rationed from a usual source, for him to go to a less usual source and get what he wants at a higher price. Nevertheless, though they interact, control through access and through price have to be distinguished.

Third, there is a contrast in effect. Controls can be sudden, intended to operate like brakes in an emergency. Or they can be gradual, inducing a slowing-down or an acceleration by degrees. The effective control should be capable of operation in both ways.

It is relevant to note that the trend of development has been away from the older method of a non-discriminating quantitative control of credit by means of interest charges led by bank rate, and towards a greater use of discriminatory controls based on deliberate selection of particular types of activity for encouragement or restraint. These operate through regulation of access to finance, coupled with tax and institutional incentives or disincentives. The objective, as one would expect, continues to be one of developing controls which can be used smoothly and gradually in anticipation of expected developments: in other words, easier acceleration and deceleration, and less driving on the brakes. These two tendencies—greater selection, and greater smoothness in operation—are not entirely consistent, and give rise to the need for a technique for handling them in a complementary manner.

2. *General Quantitative Credit Controls*

Control over the amount of credit being given by the U.K. banking system rests conventionally on the acceptance of two reserve ratios. The first is the cash ratio: cash, meaning by this notes and coin in the tills of the banks, together with their balance with the Bank of England, is kept at a level of not less than 8 per cent of total deposits. This ratio is maintained almost automatically, the amounts being replenished as required by turning other liquid assets into cash.

The operative ratio is the liquidity ratio. Liquid assets comprise—in addition to cash—money at call and short notice, and Treasury and commercial bills. The total of these assets is kept at around 30 per cent of deposits (with a minimum of 28 per cent, varying slightly throughout the year to take account of the seasonal pattern of payments). It is this latter ratio of liquid assets which should provide the basis of control. There is no longer any question of the authorities trying to exercise control by directly limiting the volume of notes issued; any attempt to do this could only create confusion.

However, when prices are rising and resources are under pressure, even the ratio of liquid assets cannot be used very effectively as a brake; at best it becomes, as it were, a speedometer. The authorities in such circumstances are bound to be on the defensive; so far from having room for manœuvre to reconstruct the debt structure in an attempt to reduce the volume of impending maturities, they are preoccupied with how to meet impending needs and maturing obligations. Their tactics on the short-term debt must be to get their Treasury bills placed weekly without having to go out of their way to supply funds to the banking system to ensure that the weekly tender is effectively taken up. Their strategy on the longer-term debt and on refunding operations is above all to build up the market in Government securities, and to increase the willingness of the general public to hold Government debt or to make use of the savings facilities.[1] Elaborate initiatives in handling the debt or in manipulating its terms are ruled out if a likely consequence is a

[1] The process is described in two articles in the *Bank of England Quarterly Bulletin*: 'The Management of Money Day by Day' (March 1963) and 'Official Transactions in the Gilt-edged Market' (June 1966).

reduced willingness of the public to hold such debt, and when an unwise move could lead to a weakening of the gilt-edged market which could immediately make necessary supporting intervention.

The possibility of monetary management, on the basis of undertakings about the level of liquid assets and of control of the type and value of public debt being made available to the market, is thus circumscribed as long as the needs of Government borrowing fluctuate. The problem will not be that of manipulating a given amount of Government debt but of handling a changing—and probably increasing—amount of debt in a developing situation. More than that: the amount of Government debt to be refinanced will depend not only on Government requirements, but also on how far private requirements may be displacing such debt from existing investment holdings. The main concern of the financial authorities may become not that of moulding the situation to better advantage, but that of placing added amounts of Government debt in such a way as to minimise the risk of repercussions.

This is only one limitation; we have seen that there are others. A second is that the control of credit-giving on the part of the clearing banks is not the same as control in respect of banks and financial institutions generally. A clearing bank may refuse an advance to a prospective borrower. But the borrower has the alternative of finding someone with a balance at a bank who is prepared to lend the money on acceptable terms. If you want to borrow money, you have the choice (a) of borrowing on overdraft, or (b) finding someone with a deposit at a bank who does not want to spend it himself and is prepared (for a suitable rate of interest) to put it at your disposal. The banks as lenders are competing with their own customers who have balances which they too could lend. Further, as long as intermediaries at one remove escape control they are in a position to organise the use of funds already at the disposal of banks' customers. A whole range of transactions can be covered through a more intensive utilisation of deposits that already exist. A business with a deposit at its bank can lend money to a finance house who will relend it, for example, to finance hire-purchase transactions. The banks are subject to competition from outside the banking system proper, since enterprising intermediaries can organise the more intensive use of existing bank deposits when it is profitable to do so.

Third, there is a problem of definition when it comes to considering an item such as 'advances'. These cover not only straightforward loans but pieces of self-liquidating business which could be handled on the basis of commercial bills eligible to qualify as liquid assets. If kept under continuous pressure to limit advances, banks and borrowers alike would have an inducement to differentiate—that is, to select business suitable for such treatment and handle it outside the category of advances.

There is moreover a more serious difficulty about treating a figure of 'advances' as something objective and consistent. When someone writes a cheque on his account, he need not have a positive balance to his credit provided he has made arrangements to overdraw. Facilities for overdrawing are not reflected in the figures; they only show the position when the payment has been made. Therefore a total of outstanding advances at one moment of time does not touch the problem of potential advances.

Indeed it would be possible to manipulate the total of advances by insisting that borrowers from a bank borrowed the money they needed in lump sums placed to their credit, instead of using overdraft facilities. The use of the former would make the total of advances (and of deposits themselves) that much larger. At a later stage, by switching to overdrafts, the total could be made to look smaller.

The reservations which have been set out in respect of the advances figure do not invalidate the mechanism of the liquidity ratio, but they do explain its limitations and why it should need supplementing.

It has in fact been supplemented in at least two ways which, though of general application, are flexible in use. The first of these is the use of special deposits. This requires a special deposit equivalent to a given proportion of total deposits to be made at the Bank of England. These special deposits are not counted as a 'liquid asset'. The proportion thus called up can be varied. This procedure is the British equivalent of the variable reserve ratio of other countries.

The other method is even more direct: a request—in practice an instruction—such as that the banks should not increase their advances by more than a given amount in a given period, such as say 5 per cent over the next twelve months. This is a powerful supplement to any convention about reserve ratios, though it still comes up against the disadvantage that figures of total advances are susceptible to some manipulation. There is the further point that it is much more difficult to apply require-ments of this sort to non-clearing banks, since their conventions and practices are different.

It may be convenient at this point to recapitulate and to recall the three stages through which the concepts of controlling mechanisms have passed.

Stage 1 is that of the 8 per cent (as it is now) cash ratio: the concept that since money in the tills of the clearing banks and their balances at the Bank must be kept at a minimum level, and the authorities can always sell securities to the public and thereby reduce the supply of cash in this sense, they have it in their power to control credit-giving by the banking system as long as the ratio is maintained. The major difficulty over this is that if the authorities tighten up, it is the Government which in effect is forced into the Bank: Treasury bills are the most convenient liquid assets, and if more money is needed it is Treasury bills that are allowed to run off and are not replaced. Commercial borrowing is more or less insulated, and at one remove. The authorities conceded this argument when arrange-ments were brought into being for the market 'to cover the tender' with its implied commitment that funds would be provided to enable it to do so.

Stage 2 is that of the liquidity ratio: the concept that the equivalent of at least 28 per cent of deposits should consist of assets in liquid form, strictly defined. This seemed to point the way to a new type of open-market operation: one had the choice, taking the volume of outstanding Government debt as something given, of varying the extent to which it was in liquid or non-liquid form. The authorities could seek to control the position by substituting long-term securities for Treasury bills, thereby reducing the ease with which the liquid base could be built up, or of doing the reverse if one wanted to ease credit conditions. In effect, one could fund or unfund, and in the process bring restrictive or non-restrictive pressures to bear. This logically thought-out concept encountered the practical difficulty that with rising prices and heavy requirements from the public sector the authorities were not in a position to choose between short- and long-term borrowing: had they attempted to do so the gilt-edged market could have been in danger of collapse. The authorities have had to play along with the market as best they could, with little room for manœuvre, let alone effective control, under conditions of pressure.

So we are led to stage 3: to special deposits to sterilise excess reserves—very like a variable reserve ratio—and to ceilings on advances. These measures have proved effective so far as they go, but the control is still faced with how to exert pressure on non-clearing banks and financial intermediaries hidden away (as it were) at the back of the class. These are to some extent specialists, and so we shall find the authorities developing discriminatory controls to deal with special types of activity.

Some critics have sought to suggest that the traditional methods of control have been abandoned too easily.[1] Stage 2 methods as described above may be ineffective, but stage 1-type methods should—it is argued—give effective results if applied with determination. This involves allowing interest rate movements

---

[1] W. T. Newlyn, 'The Supply of Money and its Control', *Economic Journal* (June 1964); R. L. Crouch, 'The Inadequacy of "New Orthodox" Methods of Monetary Control', ibid. (December 1964).

free play, and abandoning the policy of stabilising rates and ensuring in advance that the tender for Treasury bills will be covered. An appropriate volume of Treasury bills—sufficient not only to meet public requirements but also to absorb excess bank liquidity—would be offered; the rate would go up in the market (and bank rate would be put up with it); the higher the rate went the more outside money, such as inactive bank deposits, funds lent to intermediaries, currently accruing funds, would be attracted to the market until the deficiency in the supply of money to take up bills from banks themselves was made good from other sources. As such private-sector funds were sucked in by the higher rates, financial institutions would be short of money to lend and the necessary contraction would be brought about. All that is required is courage, patience and a willingness to see short-term interest rates fluctuate freely and go to high levels as needed. An incidental effect would be that the pressure would come not only on the main banks but also on intermediaries which would be losing deposits to this reactivated bill market.

The argument above may be somewhat simplified, but it is not—one hopes—unfairly set out as regards the central core. Leaving aside the question of whether such movements of rates as seem to be called for might not create damaging disturbance, one must begin by asking where the funds will come from in response to what in essence would be an attempt by the authorities to outbid other borrowers. That they should successfully *outbid* others is central to the argument. Who are those who are to be outbidden?

To begin with, it would seem the clearing banks, with their time depositors earning interest at 2 per cent below bank rate. However, there is a difficulty here. As rates rise, so does bank rate, and therefore also the rate paid to depositors, except that relatively the deposit rate rises even more, for a 2 per cent differential when bank rate is at 5 per cent is much greater than 2 per cent differential with bank rate at 10 per cent. (If you are only getting 3 per cent but can get 5 you will have a stronger inducement to change the location of your deposit than if you were getting 8 and could get 10.) If a market in short-term Government securities is to suck in funds at the expense of other borrowers, it must offer relatively greater inducements and that is just what it does not do not only in respect of the clearing banks but also over a wide range of the field. The non-clearing banks, the financial houses, the local authorities, will all raise their rates in order to prevent themselves from being outbid. Of course some institutions might be left behind: the Post Office Savings Bank, Savings Certificates, some other facilities for National Savings, possibly the building societies who are slow to move. But when all is said, many of those whose rates are immovable or sticky are Government institutions, and therefore do not meet the case. One cannot look to an easy flow of funds being attracted from domestic sources in a response to a rise in money-market rates.

Nor can one look for a sharp contraction in demand from the users of funds in response to increased interest rates alone. Some reduction in the holding of physical stocks and a fall in house-building if the building societies lose funds; but for the rest, demand will be inelastic, at least in the short run.

There is left, however, one source of finance: higher interest rates might well attract funds from abroad. As we shall see later, such forces have been at work already. But this will do nothing to aid credit control, and in due course could serve to weaken control of the exchange position.

One is impelled to the conclusion[1] that there is no way out by going back to stage 1.

One is further left with the consciousness of the limitations of any method of *general* credit control, whether falling under the head of stage 1, stage 2 or stage 3. In any case such control is subject to the disability that it is indiscriminating in its effects on

---

[1] See M. V. Posner, 'Competition in Lending and Monetary Policy', *The Banker* (March 1961), and A. B. Cramp, 'Control of the Money Supply', *Economic Journal* (June 1966). The case as developed above owes a debt to the arguments set out in these articles.

institutions in a given category, and may not apply at all if an institution does not fall into that category. The real reinforcement has come in the use of selective controls, which discriminate between different types of activity, and are a more flexible instrument.

Before turning to discriminating controls, one further limitation deserves mention. It concerns the process of funding as applied to the private sector. It centres on irregularities in the rate at which businesses can obtain permanent finance to pay off bank borrowings. Once a successful enterprise has seen its overdraft grow through being called on to finance increasing business, a point comes where it can usefully increase its permanent capital. It is natural, therefore, for bank overdrafts in due course to be funded. This funding process serves a necessary purpose: it gives the undertaking assurance that it cannot be subjected to unexpected financial pressures; it provides the public and the institutions with securities suitable for investment portfolios for both income and growth, at a time when investments of this type are needed and suitable; and it eases the position of the banking system by enabling advances to turn over. While the concept of funding is well understood in respect of gilt-edged, where it means substituting longer-term fixed-interest obligations for early-maturing ones, it is not in the same way a conscious objective of monetary policy when it comes to facilitating equity capitalisation in the private sector of the economy. Conscious decisions by the authorities that there may be a particular time when pressure should be directed to reducing the advance business of the banks while at the same time stimulating the provision of equity finance are not a feature of the financial scene.

The neglect of this aspect of financing seems to come from the institutional character of the British financial machine. The banks do not as a rule take a direct interest in promoting new issues. Nor have they facilities for nursing companies which need equity finance but are not yet ripe for a full Stock Exchange issue. The conventional division of labour between the

institutions leaves the banks with fixed-interest lending, and
quite other institutions as holders and purveyors of shares. The
gap between the two is intended to be bridged by the issuing
houses, but in this they are intermediaries interested in floating
new issues rather than in investing funds. The hiatus becomes
more obvious in a world where prices generally are tending to
rise year by year, and where equity finance in greater amounts
and over a wider field may be the desired answer. The obstacle
to this is the inability of the banks to recognise the situation and
evolve methods of dealing with it, which means evolving a
technique by which short-term debt is nursed so that in due
course it can be placed in the form of equity finance. This
obstacle is reinforced by the existence of traditional issuing
houses thinking in terms of public issues which can be quickly
underwritten and disposed of.

What this argument envisages is a quicker throughput:
advances crystallising with the help of the banks into participating capital as a regular process, and the banks making arrangements to hold these obligations until the time is ripe to place
them with insurance companies and investment institutions, or
directly on the Stock Exchange. This could help to provide a
supply of equity investments in a world where it is natural to
demand more and more of such investments. It will also reduce
congestion and distortion in the sphere of bank advances. It is
not easy for a bank to operate a rational policy of rationing
advances in the selection of new business—for which advances
are intended—if it is preoccupied and inhibited by the existence
of outstanding advances to worthy borrowers which are ripe for
permanent financing. If the flow of permanent capital is cut off,
and the banks have both to look after their existing clients and
to meet the essential requirements of new borrowers, the problem of selection in the light of overall instructions becomes
almost impossible to administer.

But the case for bridging the gap between bank lending and
the Stock Exchange has long been put on broader grounds[1]

[1] See also Grant, *A Study of the Capital Market*, chaps. xii, xv.

apart from that of the dislocation being caused to the financial machine through the undermining of fixed-interest lending by rising prices. Already in 1909 a writer in *The Times* was recommending 'several industrial banks on continental lines, with a paid up capital of five to ten millions each'—not less than £25 to £50 million at today's prices. In 1918 a Government committee recommended facilities similar to those provided by German banks. Force of circumstances has from time to time secured some modest developments, but the banks have maintained their position unchanged: they do not participate in industrial enterprise.

3. *Discriminatory Credit Controls*

General credit controls are supported by controls bearing on particular sectors of the economy. Certain forms of activity are selected as objects of restraint, and others for encouragement.

The most important of these controls is that exercised by the Bank of England through its instructions (technically 'requests') to banks and other institutions as to how their lending policies should be conducted. It may be that loans for the purposes of personal consumption are to be refused or discouraged. The same might apply to finance for speculative property development or for purely financial operations, or for covering imports. Such instructions might be qualified, however, to allow more latitude for domestic housing. Again, certain types of business could be singled out for favourable treatment: for example exports, and productive investment in directions where capacity is short and where quick results might be expected in the way of an increase in productivity. The instructions will vary with the circumstances.[1]

Such instructions are given with the approval of the Government. In addition, the Government on its own account may intervene to hold back or stimulate particular types of activity.

[1] See text of instructions on 'Credit Restraint in 1967/68' in *Bank of England Quarterly Bulletin* (June 1967).

The control of terms of hire-purchase transactions is one example. Statutory controls lay down the minimum initial deposit and the maximum period for which credit under hire-purchase may be extended, and both deposit and period may be varied. This control particularly affects the motor industry, and also durable household goods.

Tax concessions are another powerful weapon. The owner-occupier is favoured by having his house free of any assessment for income-tax purposes, while at the same time finance through building societies is kept at a high level through special arrangements by which money deposited with them is exempt from income tax (though not from surtax). There are other methods which have been or could be used to increase the sale of houses —for example arrangements designed to reduce the scale of initial deposits—but can hardly be taken much further as long as the demand for houses tends to outrun supply, making further stimulus on the demand side inappropriate.

Lastly, there are special concessions for investment and for exports. Cash investment grants and initial allowances provide a direct encouragement to capital development. Exporters are encouraged by tax rebates and also by far-reaching credit facilities provided through the banking system in conjunction with cover given by the Export Credits Guarantee Department. The effect of these measures is to relieve exported goods from the impact of internal taxes, and to make finance available freely and cheaply so as to make possible attractive credit terms to buyers overseas.

These various devices have developed in answer to particular situations: to prevent demand for cars becoming excessive and making the home market too attractive; to restrain property speculation when there is pressure on the building industry; to combat a housing shortage; to increase industrial capacity through investment, and exports through making exporting more remunerative. Such measures supplement or mitigate general credit controls. But they are all the outcome of attempts to deal with particular problems as they arise.

4. Control and Money Rates

Discussion of control so far has in the main been in quantitative terms. It is concerned with the way in which the scale of finance, whether in general or in particular directions, can be kept within desired limits. The question of price—that is, of interest rates—has been kept subordinate, the assumption being that changes in amount will be reflected in changes in price. It remains necessary to look at the cost of money more directly. One must ask how far induced increases or decreases in money rates will of themselves influence economic activity, and—following on this—how far money rates could be managed in such a way as to become an instrument for control purposes.

Obligations entered into between lenders and borrowers or investors and enterprises involve a wide range of returns. At one extreme the return in money put on current account with banks is zero. At the other, the effective rate paid by buyers of goods on hire-purchase is around 20 per cent. (Moneylenders' rates would be even higher.) In between, with bank rate at—let us assume—6 per cent, the rate charged to borrowers by banks would normally be 7 per cent or a little more, and Government long-term borrowing rates could be between 6 and 7 per cent, while Government short-term rates would be a little below bank rate.

This relates to lending on fixed-interest terms. But the opportunities offered in the market for ordinary shares are also relevant—they are an alternative outlet for someone who wants to put his savings to profitable use—and there a yield of 5 to 6 per on the basis of current distributions and/or 10 per cent or thereabouts on the basis of earnings (that is, reckoning that retained profits also increase the value of the shareholder's holding) would be not untypical of a reasonably priced share in a company of standing. It should be added that the directors of such a company, if they were contemplating extending their business and calculating what return would make a particular piece of expansion worth while, would probably be looking for a possible return of around 20 per cent unless there were other good reasons which made the expansion necessary.

It is clear from this last example that in the case of productive investment one cannot take for granted that changes in interest rates by themselves are likely to have a direct effect on decisions concerning expansion. If the return on the prospective development is expected to be approaching 20 per cent, one cannot see movements in lending rates in a range between 5 per cent and 8 per cent as being in themselves of critical importance when it comes to reaching decisions. The tax relief allowed on bank interest further reduces the effective range.

But there are some important indirect effects. If the rise in rates is thought to be temporary, it may well pay to wait until the borrowing and subsequent funding can be made on more favourable terms; to pay 1 per cent more on a short-term loan may be relatively light, but to enter into a contract for a number of years to pay 1 per cent more than would otherwise be necessary is to accept a much more serious burden. At the same time, if rates have just risen sharply, it is not improbable that the values of Stock Exchange securities will be down; if such securities have to be disposed of to mobilise some of the funds required, this means taking a loss which delay would avoid. The liquidity arguments reinforce the case for delay; once the lower rates return not only will long-term borrowing be cheaper, but any assets available for realisation will bring in more. Further, the mere tightening of rates may raise misgivings as to how far the development might be hampered by difficulties in raising enough funds to carry it through. Investment projects can require considerable sums of money to be raised over periods of time; one can never be absolutely certain that these will be forthcoming when needed in the amounts required; a period of rising rates must raise some doubts and provide arguments for delay on this account also.

It will be noted that all these considerations—fear of entering into long-term obligations at higher rates than may be necessary, depreciated state of existing assets, fear that the flow of finance will not be maintained—are cumulative. They reinforce each other in the direction of postponing those parts of investment plans that can easily be postponed without danger to existing activities. Nevertheless their force is transitory. Once the higher rates have been established, and there is no expectation of an early reduction, and once the flow of finance at the higher rates has shown itself to be uninterrupted, much of the force in the arguments for waiting disappears. After all, the difference between 20 per cent and 7 per cent is substantial, and with no immediate prospect of it getting even wider, the case reasserts itself for going ahead.

Productive investment in income-producing assets provides the most important illustration of how interest-rate changes affect economic activity. The extreme contrast is that of borrowing and lending for financial purposes: in effect, the manufacture of liquidity. Here the matching of interest rates paid and received in respect of various sums of money is central: the margins may be very narrow; an institution borrows at one rate for one period and lends at another for another; it can do so because there are many of these transactions going on at the same time; it must watch the liquidity position and the composition of its assets and liabilities with the utmost care. Rate changes—in particular, relative changes—do have very important effects, and can lead to a large fluctuation in the volume of business which can be safely undertaken.

Yet when we come to the end-product of these financial operations—funds available to productive enterprise for investment purposes—the immediate impact is likely to be not so much a change in the cost of the money but rather in the amount of the money available. We are back where we started. Facing his bank manager or financier, the prospective borrower will be less concerned over the cost of the money as over how much of it he will be allowed at the going rates. The borrower might well be anxious to use much more—but he is rationed by the lender.

The same phenomenon is to be observed elsewhere in the economy: the ultimate user of finance cuts down his plans for spending not because money has become too dear but because he cannot get as much of it as he could use. Even a cut-back in Government expenditure will generally be due not to the exhaustion of suitable purposes on which it could be used, but because the pressure on the economy is such that as a matter of policy some pieces of expenditure have to be postponed or abandoned. Similarly with building societies. As a matter of policy they are slow in changing both the rates they offer to those who put money with them and the rates they charge to those who borrow money from them to buy houses. The result is that when the opportunities for getting higher rates of interest elsewhere are increased (and building society rates do not follow), the flow of funds coming to the societies falls off, and they have to cut back the scale of their lending. Here again a change in price translates itself into a change in amount; the potential demand for houses is there, but the societies have to ration borrowers.

It is much the same with short-term borrowing. Distributors and retailers with stocks have a substantial mark-up and quick turnover; the cost of finance in respect of each article sold is small. In a world of rising prices, it would pay to keep large stocks in a great many standard lines, in anticipation of rises. That this does not happen is due less to the cost of money than to the unwillingness of bank managers to cover more than reasonable amounts. A higher charge for bank loans could not be relied on to choke off demand by itself.

If one looks at the rate structure as a whole, the process involved might be described as follows. Some rates move much more easily than others. Bank rate can be moved freely by the authorities. Certain other rates follow it automatically. Others do so after special action has been taken, or after an interval. Others move only slowly. Some do not change at all. The displacement of some rates while others remain unchanged has repercussions on the flow of funds. The amounts available are reduced in certain directions. An increase in short-term rates leaves longer-term markets short of money, and the volume of new issues which the stock markets can absorb is lessened. The changes in rates relatively to each other have affected the volume of funds coming forward in response to the various types of return, and a process of rationing and postponement adjusts the demand to the new conditions of supply.

This relates to the mechanics of the matter. There still remains the question of the objective to be sought in the application of interest-rate policy. There are four possibilities, and they have to be reconciled, as they do not pull in the same direction.

These objectives can be set out fairly simply as follows:

(i) *Steady increase in production and maintenance of reasonably high level of employment.* This objective would be favoured by steady rates, avoiding sudden changes. As long as resources are fairly fully engaged, the rates can be expected to stand at a reasonably high level, as a measure of restraint on excessive demand.

(ii) *Minimising the cost of Government debt.* This by itself is clearly favoured by keeping rates as low as possible.

(iii) *Attraction of foreign funds to London.* With heavy deficits on the balance of payments special steps may be necessary, and this will involve rates on the high side to outbid the attractions of rival financial centres abroad. But one must also add that sudden jumps of bank rate to abnormally high levels could create alarm and despondency, and even the withdrawal of funds in face of what could look like panic measures.

(iv) *Securing necessary fixed-interest finance in face of rising prices.* If prices are expected to go on rising, and new long-term money is to be found for necessary purposes, the rate of return must be high enough to compensate for falling purchasing power and to allow an effective return in real terms.

Of these, (ii) and (iv) are in conflict, and as long as prices are rising and net borrowing is required, (iv) must largely prevail. Under circumstances of full employment and utilisation of resources, (i) also favours rates at a relatively high level, as does (iii). The prospects of cheap money are at present pretty remote.

But—looking back to the inter-war period and drawing the moral—it would be well to remember that if we were to find ourselves in a world of under-employment and falling prices, the conclusions to be drawn would be the exact opposite. Such a world would call for cheap money and a policy of increasing liquidity, and the problems of restraint would be out of the way.

5. Some Implications of Control

The discussion so far has been in terms of financial control. Such an approach must not be allowed to obscure the importance of fiscal measures: the effects on the economy of changes in the flow of Government expenditure. It is necessary to correct the balance.

To say this is not to deny the importance of the financial structure as such, and the way that the machine is operated. The collapse of the banking system in the United States in the crisis of 1932 is a spectacular reminder of what grave consequences can arise. Admittedly, that is an abnormal case. On a lower plane, major economic policies can be frustrated through a failure of the financial machine to respond, or—in the opposite sense—through too active and uncontrolled a response, which can generate excess liquidity and lead to an overheating of the economy. Unwelcome side-effects can ruin otherwise sensible measures.

Nevertheless the power of the Government in controlling the flow of income and demand through its expenditure and taxation policy is so great that it should predominate in any assessment.

The Government spends; and it raises money through taxes. The scale on which it does both is very large, and has a corresponding influence. If there is slack in the economy, spending can fruitfully be increased and/or taxes reduced. The increased flow of income thereby generated in the community will, if carried far enough, take up the slack. In the converse case, a reduction in the flow of income being generated by the Government will take the pressure off an economy which is in danger of being over-extended.

The process can be followed step by step. An additional sum of money, spent on engaging labour or acquiring supplies, sets in train a flow of demand. The original additional expenditure will be passed on in part, in diminishing amounts, as only part will be spent at each stage. The final effect on income will be larger than the initial effect, since we have to add to the latter the sum total of the amounts which will have been added to the incomes of the later recipients at each stage as expenditure goes on its way.

The relationship between the initial effect and the final outcome is that of the Multiplier, a concept first elaborated by Richard Kahn in 1931 in the context of unemployment.[1] In the original presentation—evolved in terms of a world of heavy unemployment—the starting-point was the initial expenditure required to set one man to work, and led to such questions as to how much further employment would be created when the consequent further expenditure in due course had its full effect. (Keynes's view was that the original figure should be multiplied by $1\frac{1}{2}$ or 2; on a 'conservative' estimate he reckoned that for every two men brought directly into employment, one further man at least would in due course find work.)

In present conditions, with unemployment no longer the dominant problem that it was, the same approach can be

---

[1] In the *Economic Journal* (June 1931). These ideas were the subject of four articles by Keynes in *The Times* in March 1933, and those in their turn were enlarged into a pamphlet: J. M. Keynes, *The Means to Prosperity* (Macmillan, 1933).

applied more appropriately in terms of money flows. This has the further merit that one can start with the extra spending as a net addition (for example, over and above any savings which might accrue from the reduction in payments to the unemployed). To illustrate: if an extra £100 a week is added to spending on investment or otherwise as an act of policy, in due course the addition to the total outlay of the community will be £300 if the division is two-thirds spent and one-third saved.

This of course is only an arithmetical example, to bring out the basis of the calculation, which is that, assuming that we have a satisfactory measure of the propensity to consume, the ultimate increase in the National Product is the initial injection multiplied by the reciprocal of the amount withheld from further spending at each stage. The example does not tell us anything about how long it will be before the effects of the additional spending have worked themselves out. And of course the proportion being spent will vary according to circumstances.

Such an example assumes other things remaining equal. This may seem reasonable as long as the figure remains at £100, but obviously if it became £10 million a week things cannot remain equal; a lot of changes must be set in motion. These changes may be delayed as long as there are unused resources—human and material—which can be brought into production. But as soon as the flow of spending power begins pressing on the economy, things begin to happen. Once the productive system is unable to meet added demands at the existing level of prices, (a) imports from abroad will start coming in to meet the demand, (b) prices will rise, and (c) there will be an inducement for producers to expand capacity to meet this new demand. The greater the pressure on productive capacity, the more these forces will show themselves. On the other hand, a modest increase in demand could act as a modest stimulus to producers, who might be able to expand demand without undue difficulty, and with profit to themselves. So the scale of this new demand becomes important in itself; a change in size becomes a change in kind.

The three consequences listed above deserve some further attention. (*a*) is self-explanatory: increased demand which cannot be met from increased supply will involve either imports from abroad or—with not dissimilar effects—reduced exports, since goods which would otherwise have been sold abroad are consumed at home. (*b*) on the face of it is self-explanatory also, but one should note that the rise in prices can go further than appears on the surface. Prices start by rising because of the increased demand; but very soon the rise in prices can be followed by a rise in money wages which in turn will react on prices, and so on cumulatively.

But (*c*) is an equally significant phenomenon. An increase in the flow of expenditure, once it has passed a certain point, will call for an increase in productive capacity. But such an increase is costly to undertake, and brings in its return only subsequently, and then over an extended period of time. We thus arrive at the position that once the flow of effective demand gets beyond the point where existing resources are fully in use, new investment is called for. This investment may involve a once-and-for-all cost of four or five times the amount of annual spending power for which it is designed to cater. The relation between the addition to income and the investment expenditure to which it gives rise in order to provide a corresponding flow of goods is an accelerating one. A sudden increase in demand which presses on capacity, and so makes new investment necessary to increase capacity, will make for a quite disproportionate enlargement of the load which the capital-goods industries— geared otherwise largely to replacement work—have to bear. Pressures on the accelerator lead to great swings in the demand for capital goods.

To summarise the process of expansion, increased expenditure will have a multiple effect to the extent that increased income is passed on in further spending. A growing flow of expenditure will gradually press on the limits of productive capacity. To enlarge productive capacity will call for large once-and-for-all outlays on investment until capacity and output are increased. During this investment phase there will be a very large increase in the demand, e.g., for machines, since the machine-making industries will be dealing not only with their normal replacements but with a sudden added demand for the expansion.

To complete the picture: if the process is the opposite and outlay is falling, the acceleration process will work in the opposite direction and carry with it a fall in the output (and outlay) of the investment industries, while the consequent reduction in the flow of expenditure will diffuse itself. The Multiplier will begin work in reverse.

Looked at in this way, two limiting factors become apparent. The first is the extent to which there are unused resources. The second is the significance of the scale of operation of the industries producing investment goods, and how quickly and to how great an extent they can bring themselves to increase capacity. A process of expansion which works within these limits can lead to a steady and effective increase in production. One which overruns them leads to dislocation.

Fiscal policy therefore must seek to keep effective demand at an appropriate level. It can do so most simply by working on the flow of general spending as a whole. But a more refined approach needs to distinguish between expenditure for consumption purposes and for investment. If the problem is one of too much expenditure pressing on productive resources, the effective answer is to cut back on consumption expenditure but to encourage expenditure on investment in order to enlarge productive capacity. Recent taxation changes—in particular, the introduction of the corporation tax—appear to be intended to prepare the way for this. In theory it might be possible, when the economy is overheating, to increase income tax and to reduce corporation tax, thereby stimulating investment at the expense of consumption.

In the reverse case, if investment were going ahead too fast, such machinery could be used for encouraging consumption and discouraging new investment. In place of general squeezes and general relaxations, the way is open to encouraging shifts from consumption to investment and vice versa, instead of treating both alike.

It is into this picture that financial controls have to fit. How do they look against this background, the main feature of which is that the management of economic affairs by budgetary means has become the major force in promoting stability and continuity?

First, quantitative controls. These operate on liquidity through control of credit, and must continue to have their part to play whether by operating on the banks' liquid assets in the ordinary way, or taking the form of additional special deposits. It must be conceded, however, that they are indiscriminate in their operation. It is for this reason that they are best used when their use is foreseen and made manifest, and in these circumstances they have a limited power. They have a much greater and much more dangerous degree of power if they are used as a weapon of surprise. Such use may become necessary as a method of dealing with an emergency which should not have been allowed to arise, but they lead to stop–go effects which dislocate production, retard efficiency, and in the extreme could create economic stagnation.

Second, the part played by the money market in the control of credit is open to some question. The development of new short-term money markets, in particular for local authority finance and in respect of hire-purchase business, providing rates of return out of line with short-term Government rates, may have some use in attracting volatile foreign money, but seem difficult to justify. The desirability of structural changes in the money market must come into consideration, and this would have to take in the whole problem of peripheral public-sector borrowing.

Third, techniques of discriminatory control. Different parts of the economy have very different problems. Discriminatory techniques will have to be developed, whether by way of 'request' or by way of tax or other concessions. The question here is how far it will be possible to secure a more effective combination of clarity and flexibility.

Fourth, the problem of 'funding', though in fact it goes deeper than this. In a world of rising prices, the whole future of long-term fixed-interest lending must be in some doubt. As long as the upward pressure on prices continues, large parts of the economy are becoming more and more dependent on equity capital, which gives some protection from the automatic loss due to the fall in the value of money. The unimpeded flow of short-term obligations into marketable securities becomes important. But the flow stops with the banks, who still have no direct responsibility even for facilitating the process by which expanding enterprises can turn their short-term obligations into permanent capital, much less the equity capital which is needed. This field remains abandoned to issuing houses, working in haphazard competition with each other.

Fifth, interest rates. It may not be possible to do much to reduce them in present circumstances. Nevertheless, it would be of great benefit to the economy if they could be kept more stable. The U.K. is a great trading and financial centre, with large Government expenditures to be passed across the exchanges in addition. In such circumstances interest rates must be exposed to some pressure from abroad. But one is bound to ask whether a greater measure of insulation might not be desirable and practicable.

All these are directions which it could be rewarding to explore. Before doing so—bearing in mind in particular the problems of the United Kingdom—there are international implications to be examined.

CHAPTER SIX

The External Position of Sterling

1. *The Components of the External Balance*

Geography and history have seen to it that British interests and influences do not begin and end at the coasts and ports. We trade with the rest of the world, and are debtors and creditors on a world scale. More than this, sterling is an international reserve currency, which finances not only our domestic economy and our own dealings with others, but also dealings between other countries where the United Kingdom is not directly concerned. When things are going well, these wide connections are a source of strength. When they are not going well—as we have learned—it can be very much otherwise.

The U.K. balance of payments with the rest of the world can for broad purposes most easily be understood in its simplest form under four heads:

(i) *Current commercial account*. This covers receipts from exports and payments for imports; receipts and payments on services; the current earnings from our existing investments and the current outgoings on investments of others with us.

(ii) *Government account*. We have very substantial military outlays overseas, and the costs of an elaborate diplomatic and representational system all over the world to meet. Payments have to be made for political reasons. Against this there may be some receipts by way of support costs or otherwise, but they are likely to be small in comparison.

(iii) *Investment account*. We are constantly adding to our permanent investments abroad. In their turn other countries are adding to such investments in the United Kingdom. We cannot be certain how the balance will go at any point of time. Investments in this sense are income-producing assets which are not intended to be realised easily or quickly in view of the risk of loss, since one can only dispose of an investment by finding a purchaser at a satisfactory price and there is no guarantee that such a purchaser can be found. We accept the risk of being left with the investment. This applies both to investments with others and others' investments with us.

(iv) *Short-term capital account.* This consists of claims and obligations in both directions—temporary or renewable borrowings which can be called on for payment at face value in the near future. These are liquid assets to those who are due to receive payment, and maturing liabilities to those who have to pay. The distinction between these and the investments just mentioned is of course that while there is no certainty that the investments can be realised at a satisfactory price, the short-term obligations are payable at face value.

It will be noted that the first two items—the commercial and the Government payments and receipts—are both on current account. They can be looked on as the equivalent of consumption expenditure in both directions. The last two items are on capital account; that is to say, they relate to assets and liabilities which may or may not be easily realisable. Excessive payments under the first two items would for a country be the equivalent of someone spending too much of his income and becoming poorer; on the other hand, excesses in the case of the last two items lead to the complications which arise from lack of liquidity. If we have been adding to our overseas investments too fast, we may be faced with the sort of difficulty which arises in the case of a business that is overtrading. We may be conducting—in respect of our borrowing and lending—a profitable business internationally looked at in the round, but one which may leave us short of the means of payment when we are called on to meet maturing obligations.

The four categories as set out are rough and ready. Commercial account, if we were strict in our definitions, would be confined to items for which we are actually paid, or make payment, during the period, leaving the unpaid items to be handled under short-term capital account. Government account may include items where at some late stage some repayment could be forthcoming, and to this extent one could regard it as an investment; but in practice there is no way of telling how far certain payments may take the form of loans for which in practice repayments will never be claimed. Finally, the line between investments and short-term obligations may be difficult to draw. Nevertheless, as long as these qualifications are not overlooked, it is useful and sensible to think of a balance of payments as built up of these four components.

The basic distinction is between current and capital account. A deficit on current account is a deficit quite simply. The capital-account items have to be looked at not only from the point of view of the profitability of the investments, but also of the liquidity of the assets involved and how easily they could be realised, should payments necessities call for a realisation. This suggests the warning parallel of the successful industrialist who allows himself to run short of cash to pay his wages on a Friday, and the penalties for doing so may be much the same. It is a problem of liquidity, which will be endangered if—for example —we borrow short and lend long.

To turn again to the four heads, each throws some light on the sources of Britain's external weakness.

As regards the first—current commercial account—it is in this respect that one meets the complaint that exports ought to be higher and imports less. The more penetrating criticism would be in the form that production is not rising fast enough. If output were increasing more rapidly, it would leave scope for greater exports or decreased imports (with home production displacing imports) or more probably something of both. The fundamental difficulty is that although the economy is at full stretch, productivity is not increasing as it should, having regard to the possibilities open to us and the experience of other countries. This is not to say that methods of improving facilities for exports or controls on imports should be disregarded; but how to increase production is the more fundamental long-term problem.

Turning to the second head, Government expenditure overseas may be so great that with the sort of increases in production that we could reasonably hope for we should still be in deficit on current account. This is a question of fact. If it is accepted that Government outlay overseas is more than we can bear, the only remedy is a reduction. One can go further; it could be that a disproportionate attempt to divert resources into meeting such overseas requirements is one of the factors holding back productivity.

But neither of these aspects is of direct concern here. The third and fourth heads are. Investment outlays and receipts and the movement of short-term funds are essentially matters of finance. We could well be in balance on current account commercially and have a surplus sufficient to cover the Government outlay on top of this, and yet be running into difficulties through tying up funds overseas and incurring short-term liabilities which we may be called on to meet without being able to realise the investments which they have made possible. This is the old problem of borrowing short while investing long.

We have to take account of all three sources of weakness. With the failure of productivity to rise, we are faced with the weakness on commercial account, which increased austerity may not be enough to remedy, since austerity itself may hold back production to an extent which the consequent release of labour for more productive purposes cannot compensate. Government overseas expenditure is by common consent exceedingly burdensome. But over and above this an active external financial policy can very seriously add to our weakness. Indeed we can conceive of the current account being in balance and our wealth increasing, but nevertheless find ourselves under recurring pressures on overseas payments account because of the

scale and terms on which we have allowed ourselves to incur
international financial obligations.

2. *Sterling Between the Wars: The Convertible Floating Pound*

Such difficulties are not new. The fortunes of sterling over the
last fifty years help to throw light on contemporary problems.

After the First World War, in March 1919, Government
support for the sterling exchange was withdrawn. Until then,
the rate had been pegged with the help of the banking house of
J. P. Morgan in New York. With the peg out, sterling fell from
the figure of $4.76 at which it had been held. (The pre-war
parity was $4.86⅔.) The fall was sharp and within a year the rate
was down to $3.40. It then recovered, but did not reach $4.00
until the autumn of 1921. In 1922 it was up to between $4.40
and $4.50 and reached $4.70, only to come down again to $4.20
in January 1924, when the first Labour Government came into
office with Liberal support. Throughout 1924 it was tending to
rise. This continued in 1925, and that year the pound was pegged
at the pre-war parity: 'the Norman Conquest of $4.86⅔'.[1]

Certain features of this phase should be noted. Throughout
the pound was fully convertible. Residents of the U.K. could
make payments abroad freely, and residents elsewhere could
withdraw their money freely. But until stabilisation the price
varied. If there was a demand for sterling, sterling rose and one
had to pay more dollars to acquire a given number of pounds.
If there was a demand for dollars, sterling fell and one had to
pay more pounds to get the same amount of dollars. Pressure on
sterling would be corrected through a change in the price. The
change in the rate made it worth while for those who wished to
put money outside the U.K. to wait until the rate improved.
Conversely, if sterling rose too fast, anyone who had to make

[1] Montagu Norman was the Governor of the Bank of England. The
remark is attributed to O. T. Falk, a progressive private banker. For some
account of the stabilisation see Grant, *A Study of the Capital Market*, pp. 101–8.

overseas payments had an inducement to make them forthwith
and the rise was checked. As long as the rate was free to move,
there was an element of built-in stability.

After stabilisation in 1925, the picture was different. Sterling
was still convertible but the rate was fixed within very narrow
limits. Once it moved beyond those limits, it paid to ship gold
from centre to centre. This gold was something which central
bankers and monetary authorities provided in bulk, in the form
of bullion. The exchange rates were in effect guaranteed; since a
movement against sterling could no longer be discouraged by a
movement in the rate, gold went out. A movement in favour of
sterling meant the accrual of physical gold as soon as overseas
holders had to replenish their London balances. Technically
what happened was that in 1925 private citizens lost the right to
demand gold sovereigns, but the Bank of England accepted the
responsibility of settling in gold bars.

With fixed rates, international trading was made easier and
financial business simpler, but the old protection against speculative monetary movements was gone. The speculator was in a
stronger position: he knew that if a crisis were to be followed by
devaluation, he would stand to make a large profit; if the
devaluation did not materialise, he would have the working
costs of the operation to meet, including that arising from any
improvement that might take place in the currency against
which he was speculating, but the scope of that improvement
would be restricted with fixed limits in operation. If the devaluation was expected to be at all substantial, possible gains could
heavily outweigh possible losses.

The inter-war stabilisation lasted, as far as sterling was
concerned, for six years. The Great Depression involved falling
commodity prices throughout the world, a financial collapse in
the United States and a sharp increase in unemployment in this
country. In 1929, one in ten of the working population was out
of work; in 1931 the proportion had doubled to one in five. The
international payments system broke down. In the case of
sterling the peg was pulled out in September 1931 and the

pound again floated—still convertible into foreign currencies though not into gold, but only at going rates.

The sequel was this. By the end of 1931, sterling was down (from $4.86) to $3.40. In 1932 there was improvement, but nevertheless sterling was again down to $3.40 by the end of the year. The rate was not much better at the beginning of the following April. Then on 20 April 1933 the United States went off gold, and the dollar also was floating. Eleven weeks later, sterling had risen in terms of the dollar to $4.75. By November 1933 the sterling-dollar rate had touched $5.25, well above the old parity. Sterling remained slightly above the old parity for the best part of five years, till the autumn of 1938, when the activities of Hitler's Germany led to a fall with the fears of war to come.

The great swings of the earlier years following immediately on 1931 had some disadvantages, but they evoked technical devices to deal with them. From the U.K. point of view, the most important was the creation of the Exchange Equalisation Account. Its purpose was to acquire (against the issue of Treasury bills) foreign funds that came to London, and to use its foreign exchange holdings in such a way as to smooth out fluctuations. It helped to insulate the economy from the effects of sudden influxes and withdrawals of hot money, and steadied the rates. But there was no limit on the actual exchange rates within which it was expected to operate, and it was therefore in a position to deal with large movements of foreign balances into and out of London.

The freedom given by the abandonment of the fixed exchange in 1931 had one important indirect consequence. As long as the parity was fixed, interest rates in London were closely bound up with interest rates elsewhere. But once an element of insulation was introduced by a movable rate, the authorities were enabled to put through a major conversion operation on War Loan, and to introduce a policy of cheap money which cleared the ground for some attack on unemployment. External insulation gave a breathing space for internal relief.

At the same time the readjustments which had taken place

had wider consequences in more distant parts. The rise in the price of gold meant that private holdings of gold jumped in value, and gold came out of hoards releasing finance for productive use, of especial help in underdeveloped countries. Private individuals had funds to invest once they had disposed of their gold holdings. The gold accrued to monetary authorities, and this added strength allowed them to adopt a more forward-looking and less apprehensive attitude towards economic expansion. Finally, the enhanced price of gold—the United States had revised its price to $35 per fine ounce in early 1934—meant greater liquidity for reserve-holding institutions since it left them with the possibility of revaluing their own holdings. The U.K. rebuilt her gold reserves not only through a strengthened balance of payments, but because of the flow of gold from the East (which came not only to settle current payments but also on capital account), while the physical value of gold per unit went up in terms of pounds.

Yet this account of what happened in the 1930s should end on a cautionary note. Sterling went down after September 1931, and then began to rise. At that point in particular its buoyancy owed something to the spare capacity and unemployed resources which could be brought into play on any downward movement. If British prices became lower in comparison with those in other countries, our exports were in a position to increase, and home production could displace imports. This was an important reinforcement. No such reinforcement is available to a country which floats when its manpower and other resources are extended, and the freeing of resources to take advantage of the new opportunities becomes a matter of urgency and difficulty.

3. *Sterling After 1945: Fixed Exchanges and Convertibility for Non-Residents*

After 1945 the position of sterling was very different. In the twenty years from 1919 to 1939, sterling had floated for two-thirds of the period, and was stabilised for the remaining third. Throughout, the pound was convertible into other currencies for residents and non-residents alike. In the twenty years from 1946, the pound has been stabilised (with a devaluation from one fixed rate to another in 1949) but convertibility has been restricted to non-residents. Payments by U.K. residents to persons outside the Sterling Area have remained subject to exchange-control permission except for current commercial transactions.

The reasons for these changes are to be found in monetary history and monetary practices. The main innovation in practice was the systematisation of the techniques of exchange control during the war. These were effective as long as an active control of trade and scrutiny of payments were essential for the prosecution of the war. With peace, the relaxation and even disappearance of control over trading operations reduced very sharply the effectiveness of exchange control. This was especially so with the U.K., which had its special relationship with the Sterling Area. The distinction between residents of the U.K. and residents outside both the U.K. and the Sterling Area was extremely difficult to handle as a basis of exchange-control policy; it would have been difficult enough if the problem had arisen from a straightforward line drawn between residents and non-residents of the U.K.

This difficulty was reinforced by the existence of a fixed rate. A floating rate provides a built-in protection against movements of hot money getting out of control. But the problem goes much wider than that of speculative movements of funds in search of a capital gain or seeking to avoid a capital loss. If there is fear of a devaluation, the timing of payments in respect of ordinary commercial transactions will be affected. Floating currency arrangements take care not only of speculative movements, and of hedging by overseas holders of sterling assets, but also of those 'leads and lags' associated with the timing of normal everyday payments which have to be made across the exchanges.

Such problems were not unforeseen, and an attempt was made to anticipate them through the creation at the end of the war of the International Monetary Fund and the International Bank for Reconstruction and Development. These were vehicles by which the financially stronger countries were enlisted to provide facilities for those in need of funds. The I.M.F. was in effect a banker of last resort for national monetary authorities, providing a foundation of international credit on which they could draw within carefully specified limits and subject to conditions. The I.B.R.D. (and its associated institutions) are providers of long-term capital for development purposes.

Institutions such as these, together with *ad hoc* arrangements which developed as time went on, did provide a basis on which the structure of fixed rates and non-resident convertibility was operated. But as time went on certain serious problems came into evidence, mainly arising from the position of the United States and the U.K. as suppliers of international reserve currencies. Was the I.M.F. to act as a support for the dollar and the pound to enable them to continue and expand as a medium for international transactions? If so, the Fund's policy would have to be directed to supporting them in a way different from the support given to currencies which did not have a large part to play in financing international business. Or was the role of the I.M.F. to be directed to providing a more uniform treatment to meet the normal balance of payments requirements of countries for their own needs?

The difficulties which exist between the United States and Britain on the one hand and France on the other would on analysis appear to centre on this particular aspect. This is bound to affect any international plan for promoting international liquidity. The French attitude would appear to be that the price of gold should be substantially written up; that this would provide any necessary enlargement of credit; and that the United States and Britain should set their own houses in order, which—however it was interpreted—would seem to have the incidental effect of reducing their capacity to carry out international financial operations. If so, what is to take their place?

Whether this be a fair interpretation or not, it remains that the policy of supporting a stable-rate international system on the basis of the credit-creating powers of international institutions is in serious difficulties, and this is added to by conflicts of political interest. The additional support necessary has become the subject of continuous informal negotiations and bargaining. Effective and adequate systems of international credit creation have been outlined many times on paper, but the prospect of such a system being agreed upon by the many countries needed to make it work is still far away. And without a far-reaching system of this kind, the strains and stresses of maintaining fixed rates cannot be eliminated. Movements of gold away from the United States (which in consequence is forced to restrain its international financing) and towards France and other countries which are less given to such investment seem bound to make for the contraction of international liquidity. The problems of the United States may be the larger in scale, but those of the U.K. are more immediate. It is not easy to see agreement on any set of international monetary arrangements of a kind which would enable the present fixed-rate system to be developed.

In the meantime there are outward signs of the pressure to which the existing international payments system is subject. The strongest evidence of the general lack of confidence is in the amount of gold that is going into hoards. In 1965 the supply of new gold (including Russian sales) was valued at $1,985 million. Only $400 million went to monetary authorities and other official bodies; all the rest went for 'reported' industrial use and 'private absorption'—much the larger part being private absorption. Ten years previously, out of a supply of just over $1,000 million, two-thirds had gone to official purchasers.[1]

In the U.K. other signals pointed in the same direction. One of the features of convertibility for current transactions, coupled

[1] Figures from Bank of International Settlements *Annual Report* for 1965–6. In 1966 official gold stocks failed to register any increase.

with restrictions on capital movements, is that special rates
grow up alongside the official rates. U.K. residents were allowed
—though this has been considerably restricted—to invest outside the Sterling Area to the extent that other such investments
were being realised; this led to a market where the proceeds of
realisations were sold to those who wanted to make new investments. Similarly, Americans and others who had investments in
the U.K. could only realise them to the extent that other non-
residents were prepared to take them over. The prices in the
markets of security ('switch') sterling,[1] the currency used by
non-residents to deal in British stocks, and the investment dollar,
used by residents to deal in non-residents' securities, reflected
the pressure on sterling.

A more fundamental change is the growth, in particular since
1960, of the international market in externally-owned foreign
currencies, mainly dollars. This represents a major development
with large implications, which needs to be examined separately.

4. *The International Market in Expatriate Currencies*

The most far-reaching development in the international
monetary field is the growth of dealing in currencies in centres
outside the country of origin of the currency in question. The
currency most frequently dealt in is the dollar, which one would
expect, but there are also dealings on a much smaller scale in
sterling (mainly in Paris), in Swiss francs, German marks, and
Dutch guilders. The major market is in Euro-dollars centred in
London. It dates as a market from the late 1950s and the early
1960s, following on the easing of exchange restrictions. It was
not mentioned in the Radcliffe Report.

Euro-dollars are deposits in U.S. dollars with banks—including overseas branches of American banks—outside the
United States. Such expatriate dollars can originate with holders in any country of the world; but they are largely dealt in
through European financial centres, hence the prefix 'Euro'.

[1] The security sterling market was abolished on 12 April 1967.

The holder of a dollar credit has a choice as to whether he banks it inside or outside the U.S. (This is obviously so in the case of a holder resident in a country other than the U.S., but U.S. residents also at one time held large deposits in U.S. dollars with Canadian and other foreign banks, though these are now much reduced.) The holder may deposit direct with an American bank in, say, New York. Or he may hold it as a dollar balance with a bank outside the U.S. in his own or some other country, whether it be a domestic bank or an overseas branch of an American bank. The strict definition requires that the former—i.e. direct holdings with banks in the U.S.—would not be Euro-dollars; the latter would.

However, statistically it is difficult to distinguish, for example, between dollars in New York held by European banks for their own account as working balances, and dollars held by them and reflecting the dollar deposits of their customers. A further problem of definition lies in the fact that dollars held in Europe and re-lent may pass through several hands before they reach an ultimate borrower; there has even developed in London (and elsewhere) a market in negotiable certificates of deposit denominated in U.S. dollars. Thus there are statistical difficulties both of identification and of eliminating duplication. Nevertheless, the basic concept is relatively clear: U.S. dollars dealt in outside the United States.

Business in Euro-dollars is large. The Bank for International Settlements put the size of the Euro-dollar market at $9·5 milliard at the end of March 1966.[1] This represents a rise of some $2 milliard over the previous year. If one adds the other currencies dealt with externally on a smaller scale—sterling,

[1] The main source of information on Euro-dollars is the *Annual Report* of the Bank for International Settlements, which gives figures and an analysis and account of developments in the year covered. The *Bank of England Quarterly Bulletin* gives figures of the U.K. position in respect of foreign currencies; see also the article on 'U.K. Banks' External Liabilities and Claims in Foreign Currencies' in the *Bulletin* for June 1964. Dr. Paul Einzig, *The Euro-dollar System* (2nd ed., Macmillan, 1965), has valuable information on the structure and working of the market. The latest estimate of the B.I.S. puts the Euro-dollar market up to $13 milliard in March 1967.

Swiss francs, German marks, and Dutch guilders—the total of Euro-currencies would probably have been up to $11 milliard. This is after attempting to make allowance for duplication.

At the outset one must explain why such a short-term international money market for the lending and borrowing of dollar deposits should come into being and do business on this substantial scale; one would normally expect borrowing, lending and short-term investment in dollars to take place in the United States.

At this point one must recall the fundamental consideration influencing the scale of business in any financial market: the margin between borrowing and lending. American banks paid relatively unattractive rates to foreign depositors, at any rate until recently. On the other hand the cost of borrowing from banks in the United States was high, especially when account is taken of differences in practice. Banking practice which frowns on overdrafts and lays emphasis on minimum balances makes the differences between borrowing and lending even greater than appears at first sight. This leaves room for business to be done in dollars outside the United States by institutions working on narrower margins at a time when the supply of foreign-owned dollars is being swollen by the U.S. deficit on its balance of payments.

Against this background, three particular influences have coincided to make Euro-dollar business profitable. In the first place, there are limitations on the interest which United States banks in their own country are allowed to offer to depositors. In particular Regulation Q provides that no interest should be paid on time deposits of less than thirty days, and prescribes a maximum for what can be paid for longer periods. The yield on the short-term obligations of the U.S. Government, though it has risen, is not high compared with what can be obtained elsewhere. Interest limitations and tax obligations have made it unattractive for foreign holders to employ dollar deposits direct in the United States.

The second influence is the obverse of this. It is the existence of the other remunerative outlets. American companies operating abroad as well as concerns in the United States itself find it easier or cheaper to borrow dollars back from overseas than to borrow direct in the United States, a reminder of the institutional importance of the gap between what banks are prepared to pay those customers who hold deposits with them, and what they charge to those customers who borrow from them. In practice the greater part of the dollars passing through London are on-lent as dollars to American institutions. But there are openings also in other countries, including the United Kingdom, where high returns are obtainable on short-term lending to local authorities, to finance houses for hire-purchase, and also by temporary lending to non-clearing banks.

In respect of these last developments, the two forces mentioned might not have been enough; a third influence removes the obstacle of exchange uncertainties. The gap between the lower rates at which Euro-dollars can be borrowed and the higher rates obtainable on short-term loans in sterling and other currencies is large enough to leave room for the cost of using forward exchange facilities. As long as the difference between the two rates permits the inclusion of forward exchange cover, Euro-dollars are drawn to London to take advantage of the high interest opportunities. They can be switched into sterling and the sterling covered forward to ensure no loss on the exchange. Euro-dollars thus become the equivalent of foreign-owned sterling with an exchange guarantee.

These are the essential features which make such a market possible. There are other motives which might to some extent explain why this indirect lending of dollars should be widely used. It covers up the identity of the real owner of the dollars if he has fiscal, political, exchange-control or personal reasons for wishing to remain anonymous. Such considerations may apply both to Americans in the United States lending dollars abroad, and to non-residents with dollar balances at their disposal. For such purposes an alternative to Euro-dollars would be the holding of gold, but this—though widespread—has the disadvantage that it brings in no return, is complicated, and may be of doubtful legality in the country of the holder. Nevertheless it would be wise to discount such explanations; no doubt there is some business based on ulterior motives, but the scale of the market is too great to be explained by such considerations.

When the market in Euro-dollars first got going, central banks and official institutions (national and international) charged with the holding and handling of foreign exchange appear to have been the main participants. In this earlier phase they were active in the market, redepositing spare dollar balances in order to get the benefit of the higher yields. But although such lending of available balances continued, the scale for some time did not increase and commercial banks were playing much the preponderant part. They supplied dollars deposited with them by their clients as well as excess working balances of their own not required for their immediate foreign exchange needs. Latterly—with the business becoming more profitable—official funds have again increased.

Much of the money thus passed on originates from a much wider field. According to Dr. Einzig, insurance companies are substantial lenders. International oil and tobacco interests are both lenders and borrowers. To these must be added refugee funds of various kinds, and also a substantial amount representing accumulated oil revenues from oil-producing countries. By far the greater part of the dollar funds dealt in must be assumed to be owned by non-residents of the United States, either acquired in the normal course of business, or by the sale of other currencies to the U.S. for dollars. Lending abroad by Americans is now heavily discouraged by the U.S. authorities. However, deficits on the American balance of payments have left many non-Americans who own dollars, and do not have to borrow them.

Taking the picture as a whole, a substantial contribution to the supplies of Euro-dollars comes from countries which are not a part of the Western European financial complex, and many of which rank as underdeveloped. These funds must in large part represent reserves or personal holdings in search of a higher return. But the figures below as given by the Bank for International Settlements are larger than one might have anticipated.

Net Suppliers from Outside to European Reporting Countries

	($ million)
Middle East	710
Other Western Europe (e.g. Austria and Spain)	160
Latin America	310
Others (mainly Africa and Asia)	550

(*Source:* B.I.S. Reporting Countries are Belgium, France, West Germany, Holland, Italy, Sweden, Switzerland and the U.K. Figures relate to March 1966.)

The Bank for International Settlements also gives figures for the main European suppliers of dollars. These show that in March 1966 dollar assets exceeded dollar liabilities in the case of

	($ million)
Switzerland (including B.I.S.)	1,030
Germany	340
France	390

Two changes from the previous year are noteworthy. Canada disappears from the list of substantial net suppliers, one of the consequences of the United States policy of discouraging Americans from putting their money abroad. The withdrawal of American funds placed via Canada was, however, accompanied by a compensating change; the Italian Exchange Office provided the Italian banks with over $1,000 million on a swap basis against lire, and these dollars were largely on-lent, both inside and outside Italy. As American pressure to restrain lending abroad led to higher interest rates for Euro-dollars, so the higher rates seem to have attracted new funds into the market.

Such are the sources of Euro-dollar funds, and the net

suppliers. One must next turn to the uses to which such funds are put, and the countries which make use of them.

In the first place, banks and financial institutions have a fluctuating need for dollars to bridge temporary and foreseeable gaps in their foreign exchange requirements. They may also find opportunities for arbitrage: lending and borrowing to take advantage of temporary differences in interest rates for such loans in different financial centres, and in respect of different maturities.

Second, there is a use for Euro-dollars in financing foreign trade operations. Such transactions are basically self-liquidating, in the sense that there are defined points of time at which payments for goods can be expected, giving some assurance that the means of repayment will be forthcoming at the end of a foreseeable period.

Third, banks may quite simply be borrowing in dollars abroad for the purpose of turning these dollars into domestic currencies and relending the proceeds at a profit. In the United Kingdom the main openings are to place the money with local authorities or with finance houses for hire-purchase. Elsewhere at various times an influx of funds has been used as the basis of domestic credit expansion. This has happened in Japan and in Italy, though the Italian position has recently been much strengthened.

Last (and not least), branches of American banks abroad have channelled dollars back to the United States, for the purpose of providing working capital for American business with branches overseas, as well as for financing domestic trade and security dealers. The amount of dollars of external origin put to use in the United States is large, but it cannot be assumed that the figures accurately reflect the position on Euro-dollars in the strict sense since they could include a substantial amount of working dollar balances needed for the conduct of current financial operations.

The Bank for International Settlements has figures of the dollar positions of countries outside Western Europe who are

net users of dollars. These figures (again for March 1966) are
the obverse of those given earlier.

Net Borrowers Outside Europe from European Reporting Countries

	($ *million*)
Japan	470
Eastern Europe	360
United States	2,240

Within Europe, B.I.S. figures show for March 1966 the two
main users, with liabilities exceeding assets to the extent of:

	($ *million*)
United Kingdom	560
Netherlands	210

A year earlier, the U.K. net borrowings were as high as
$1,130 million, while Italy had a net figure of $540 million,
since wiped out.

The figures which have been given, relating to March 1966,
can be interpreted as showing a distinct pattern. This takes the
following shape:

(i) The main European centres taken together were borrowers from the world outside of something of the order of
$1,730 million. They lent $3,070 million to the world
outside. The dollars came from underdeveloped countries, and from the smaller countries of Western Europe,
and from the main European countries themselves. The
amount re-lent went to the United States (largely to or
through American business operating overseas, it must be
assumed) and also to Japan and Eastern Europe.

(ii) Within the area of the main European centres, Switzerland (including the B.I.S.), West Germany and France
were net lenders to the extent of some $1,760 million,
and the U.K. and the Netherlands net users of some
$770 million.

It remains to stress that the pattern sketched above is one in terms of net positions, and in no sense a description of flows. Dollars that are lent and re-lent lose their identity. It would be quite wrong to suggest, for example, that the dollar balances of developing countries which are lent to Europe are those dollar balances which are on-lent to the United States, or to attempt to trace links of this sort. All one can say is that particular countries are net lenders or borrowers on such-and-such a scale. It is from such net positions that the pattern suggested above is derived.

Bank of England figures give information about the U.K. position in some detail. Based on these, and showing the position in $ million, the picture which emerges is this. For March 1966, the U.K. net position shows an excess of liabilities of 560, but this is up to 800 in March 1967. Constituents of the 1966 figure are net borrowings from Switzerland, including the Bank for International Settlements (915), Canada (620) and the Middle East (440). There are also borrowings from Western Europe (other than Switzerland) of 455, and from overseas sterling countries—but borrowings in dollar terms—of 290. Net lending is to the United States (1,550) and to Japan (440).

The figure of total net liabilities of 560 mentioned above is reduced if we take into account a favourable net position in respect of other foreign (i.e. non-Sterling Area) currencies of the banks. The total comes down to 210, that is £75 million. (In March 1967 it was up to £106 million.) This, it should be recalled, is the net amount owed by the banking system—outside the central reserves—in dollars and other foreign currencies.

The attraction of London for foreign funds is the opportunity for investment provided by the borrowing needs of local authorities and hire-purchase finance companies. This arises from what has become a two-tier structure of interest rates. The differences between the return on Treasury bills and on local authority deposits for three months ranged in 1966 from a little above ½ per cent to a little below 1 per cent per annum. Finance-house deposits brought in something of the order of 1 to 1½ per cent more than Treasury bills. Of course, local authority deposits are somewhat less convenient than Treasury bills and finance-house deposits a little more uncertain, but the differences in return are much more than can be explained by differences in risk; they reflect an artificial differential arising from market structure. It is this, coupled with official support given as needed to the forward exchange rate, which has enabled London to attract the business. But the process has been very heavily reinforced by the discouragement which other centres give to this sort of business in respect of their own banks.[1] London would appear to have accepted the risk that a fall in such interest rates at home, or a rise in alternative rates overseas, would carry with it an outflow of foreign funds in the absence of immediate countervailing action.

It remains to say something of the working of the Euro-dollar market itself, on which Dr. Einzig throws light. London is by far and away the most important market. Next comes Paris. There are also substantial dealings in Euro-dollars in Frankfurt, in Amsterdam, in Zürich, Basle and Geneva, in Vienna, in Milan and in some countries in the Middle East. Canada used to serve as a channel for funds from the United States placed in Europe, but restrictions in the United States have largely put a stop to this.

Banks dealing in Euro-dollars work mainly in large round amounts between each other. This is basically a wholesale market, dealing at fine rates, within the conventionally established limits between borrowing and lending rates. Foreign exchange brokers play their part in bringing together borrowers and lenders. The banks will collect dollars from their customers, and supply them to those who wish to take them up.

The common feature of Euro-dollar dealings in the several

[1] Italy, France, the Netherlands, Norway, Sweden and Austria fix limits; West Germany, Switzerland and Denmark have special reserve or deposit requirements which act as a discouragement. West Germany, Switzerland and France forbid the payment of interest on non-resident time deposits: B.I.S. *Report* for 1965–6, pp. 46–8.

centres is the emergence of a common structure of rates. Arbitrage dealings keep the rates in line between the centres, between different periods of lending, and indeed between different externally-held currencies as long as they are convertible into dollars.

A new development has been the setting-up in the middle of 1966 of a market in London dollar-negotiable Certificates of Deposit. The lead appears to have been taken by the London office of the First National City Bank, with an international firm of New York brokers[1] undertaking to maintain a secondary market. These bearer-negotiable certificates—C.D.s—are issued in multiples of $1,000 (minimum denomination $25,000) and maturities of 30, 60, 90, 120, 150, and 180 days. C.D.s are issued by London branches of issuing banks on payment of the relative dollars being cleared in New York. The C.D. certifies that there has been deposited with the London office of the named bank a given sum of U.S. dollars, and that this is repayable solely at the London office by draft or telegraphic transfer addressed to its New York office at the expiration of so many days together with interest at a given rate. Neither the deposit nor the interest can be drawn before maturity.

Such certificates 'are not offered in the United States of America or to nationals or citizens thereof'. Nor could they be of interest to 'residents' (for exchange-control purposes) of the United Kingdom. This is a market for non-residents, and for U.K. authorised banks within their exchange-control limits. Prices are quoted as of 1 July 1966 in the circular in respect of C.D.s issued by London branches of seven American banks, and there is a suggestion of more to come.

C.D.s, it is suggested, have been introduced into Europe to fill the gap between the facilities provided by the Euro-dollar deposit market and the medium- and long-term credit instruments denominated in dollars and available internationally, and it is hoped that they will attract new funds into the Euro-dollar

[1] White, Weld & Co. The information is taken from their circular dated July 1966.

market because of their ready negotiability and greater flexibility. By the end of June 1966 there were £5 million of such certificates outstanding; three months later it had risen to £45 million, and was perhaps of the order of £80 million by the end of the year.

Alongside the market in Euro-dollar deposits and C.D.s, there has been a large volume of dollar-denominated long-term borrowing by U.S. and international companies. Much of this appears to be genuinely dollar-based; for the rest, companies needing other currencies may have been prepared in effect to give a dollar guarantee in return for favourable borrowing terms. In this market, U.S. companies seem to have been securing a predominant position, in comparison with other international borrowers. Looking at the picture as a whole, it seems fair to conclude that American interests may have done much, by providing by a roundabout route remunerative employment for foreign-owned dollars arising from the deficit on the U.S. balance of payments, to reduce the immediate pressure for turning dollars into gold at the expense of gold reserves.[1]

What will be the consequences of the growth of this very large market in internationally convertible expatriate currencies, in which the dollar plays so preponderant a part?

What happens if the economic weather were to become worse? Euro-dollars have many uses, but they leave the users exposed to pressure should there be a sudden contraction in the supply. In some cases Euro-dollars may have an effect on the domestic credit base in a borrowing country and provide the foundation for further credit expansion; the risk is that withdrawal would make necessary a more than equivalent contraction. But the danger is not confined to occasions where there is an element of gearing. In other cases a sequence of lending and borrowing carries the likelihood that the obligations at the end of the chain will be on longer terms than those at the beginning;

---

[1] But with such pressure, the U.S. interests would have to find dollars to repay any loans called in to be turned into gold at the expense of the U.S. reserves.

the risk here is the familiar one of borrowing short and lending longer. Further, the convenience of being able to call on dollars to bridge gaps between offsetting transactions may have enabled institutions to carry on with smaller normal working balances; here the withdrawal of a facility would mean either the need for its replacement by larger working balances, or a reduction in the activities of the institutions concerned. To such straightforward uses must be added the possibility that Euro-dollar loans may be supporting speculative positions or caught up in even more dubious propositions, and in these cases the withdrawal of such loans might be quite as embarrassing, with consequences affecting innocent parties. One must be prepared, for all these reasons, for dangers arising from the break-up of the Euro-dollar market if the international financial position became worse. A few financial failures or threats to a currency which led to the imposition of new exchange restrictions might precipitate a chain reaction.

At this point one recalls that—in contrast to the large national money markets in New York and London—the Euro-dollar market is without a lender of last resort.

The fundamental question is: what could precipitate a movement away from Euro-dollar business and what form could this take? If the dollar were felt to be threatened, there would be a movement towards gold and towards any currencies which were thought to be unlikely to follow the dollar all the way in its downward movement. Gold hoarding is already substantial, and could increase. Holders of Euro-dollars without access to gold might prefer their own domestic currencies, in which case the dollars would be turned in to their own monetary authorities, who would be faced with the choice of holding dollars in New York or of seeking to turn them into gold through official channels at the expense of the United States gold reserves. If there were a threat to the dollar, the existence of this great volume of foreign-held dollars, after a series of liquidations of existing positions which might be very troublesome, could exert its full pressure on the United States.

This is not to say that—from the point of view of the U.S. authorities—this pressure would be any greater than that which would have come about had an equivalent amount of dollars been held from overseas directly with banks in the United States. Indeed, the uses to which the dollars have been put and the conditions attaching to their employment would serve to make them somewhat less easily available for realisation. But to the extent that they have been embodied in the financial structures of the users, the consequences to the latter of their ceasing to be available could be damaging.

One is even tempted to ask whether in the completely opposite case, an improvement in the U.S. balance of payments which put the dollar beyond doubt and led to a demand for dollars for current payments to America, there could not also be serious embarrassment because of the reduced supply of funds in the Euro-dollar market. Probably not: an easier position on the U.S. balance of payments would presumably lead to an easier movement of funds from the United States on capital account. But if the current restrictions remained after the position had improved there could be difficulties which would show themselves in the shortage of international credit, and weaknesses of other currencies. However, this is a lesser danger than that of sudden fears for the dollar.

What of the position of London, the centre of Euro-dollar dealings, in all this? As we know, sterling is an international currency subject to exchange restrictions which circumscribe residents in their dealings outside the Sterling Area, and is in present circumstances more suspect than the dollar in face of dangers of devaluation. Euro-dollars have had an opportunity of filling a gap: in effect they are the equivalent of sterling with an exchange guarantee, and are subject to similar disadvantages.

London borrows externally in terms of dollars and to a somewhat lesser extent on-lends externally in terms of dollars, thus enabling her to continue in business as a world financial centre. There will be receipts on the balance of payments to the extent that commissions are earned and the skill of the operators secures a yield higher than the cost of the money they employ. The danger is that the loans may not be sufficiently easily realisable: the assets may not be as liquid as the liabilities, either because of lending long and borrowing shorter, or because in a crisis it will be difficult to get the money in. The best we can say is that up to now the market has proved resilient; tighter money in the U.S. has led to an increase in rates and an increased supply of Euro-dollars in response.

But as we have seen, the borrowings in dollar terms exceed the lending: there is a margin which has been turned into sterling without a corresponding external asset. To this extent there is a temporary reinforcement of the U.K. reserves. The dollars may have been turned in to the central reserves in exchange for sterling, or they may have been used to make payments which otherwise would have been a call on the reserves. Either way for the moment the reserves have been strengthened, but the dollars will have been covered forward and may be recalled in due course.

The sterling part of these dollars will be employed at a profit —possibly on deposit with local authorities or finance houses where the return is abnormally high in comparison with other forms of deposit. (At times only finance-house deposits seem to have been sufficiently remunerative.) Some such rates will have to continue to be kept well up if such funds are to be retained. It is the existence of these remunerative short-term outlets that has enabled us to secure the reinforcement of the reserves, and unless we are strong enough to see the reinforcement disappear we shall have to maintain such outlets and go on supporting the forward exchange. (In contrast, as we have seen, in West Germany, Switzerland and France there are restrictions on the employment of foreign funds for internal purposes.)

As things have come to pass, dependence on such Euro-dollar support may have been unavoidable. But it is uncertain and precarious, and at the mercy of external events. The price of it is a loss of control over internal interest rates, since we cannot escape from the necessity of keeping some short-term rates at an attractively high level, and if necessary supporting the pound exchange. This is one of the penalties of operating an international banking business and an international reserve currency when one's balance of payments is liable to be in deficit and reserves are inadequate.

5. *Methods and Objectives in the International Management of Sterling*

Sterling is weak. One can trace this weakness to three separate sources.

First, the failure of productivity to rise. To say that exports should be higher or imports lower is to complain about symptoms. The impediment is that production is not rising as fast as one might hope, given what happens elsewhere. If it were rising there would be more goods available, and this would show in more being exported and/or less imported.

The second cause is the weight of Government expenditure overseas. This outlay is mainly for military or political purposes. It ranges from the maintenance of large forces in the Far East, in Aden, in Germany and elsewhere, to the purchase of aircraft and submarines and equipment from the United States at heavy cost.

The third cause is different in character: technically it might be described as a failure of liquidity on capital account. Even if we had succeeded in earning a suplus on current commercial account sufficient to cover Government expenditure overseas, we could still have run short of funds to meet our immediate commitments—rather in the way that a wealthy man can still run out of cash. Unfortunately, when a country runs down reserves (even though it may still possess large long-term investments), it may be exposed to pressure to take measures which interfere with the growth of domestic production with the consequence that the balance of payments position becomes worse rather than better.

The particular weakness of sterling on this account springs from the growth of short-term liabilities attracted in the forms of balances to this country by high rates of interest in some

short-term markets, including lending to local authorities and
to finance houses for hire-purchase.

The figures are revealing.[1] At the end of September 1966,
accepting houses and overseas banks had a total of £528 million
on short-term loan to local authorities. These institutions together draw something like 60 per cent of their deposits from
overseas, including both sterling and non-sterling countries. In
addition to this a further £310 million was at the same time
directly on deposit from overseas with local authorities (£151
million) and with finance companies (£159 million). If one
adds some allowance for the loans made by accepting houses
and overseas banks to finance houses, the total of all these
deposits would come up from the £838 million about which we
know (the 528 plus the 310) to something of the order of £1,000
million. This cannot be treated as being wholly overseas-owned,
but it is all money in which there is a powerful foreign interest,
and much of it must be highly sensitive to the relative rates of
return obtaining in world markets. And on top of this there are
other overseas funds not lent to local authorities and finance
houses which must also be sensitive.

The question is, how much in all? The figures show that in
September 1966 external dollar liabilities of United Kingdom
banks (excluding, that is, the official reserves and liabilities)
were some £180 million greater than claims, though if the
calculation is extended to include other foreign, i.e. non-
Sterling Area, currencies, the favourable balance in respect of
these reduces the shortfall to £16 million. But we cannot treat
the surplus on the non-dollar foreign currencies as likely to be
realisable and realised for the purpose of meeting dollar obligations, and even the former dollar figure of £180 million cannot
be treated as a maximum; after all, it is a net figure arrived at
after a subtraction sum where the amounts involved were very
much greater than the difference (£2,460 million liabilities less
£2,277 million claims). One must further be prepared for some

[1] They are from the *Bank of England Quarterly Bulletin* (December 1966),
Tables 10, 19 (i) and 20 (i).

of the Sterling Area money to be withdrawn and lead indirectly to a drain of gold or convertible currency. It looks as if of a total of funds with an overseas interest approaching £1,000 million loaned to local authorities and finance houses and other funds elsewhere, something not far short of half might be interest-sensitive. On this line of argument—and failing substantial unknowns in the calculation—perhaps £400 million[1] could be at stake if there were to be a big differential advantage in putting liquid funds outside the Sterling Area.

So a rise in interest rates elsewhere or a failure to ensure that forward exchange rates are not supported in such a way as to enable holders of foreign funds to cover themselves against devaluation could mean a withdrawal of money on a scale which is not comfortable to contemplate. We can thus be faced at a time when economic developments are otherwise in our favour with the necessity of seeing very large losses from our reserves, or of forcing up domestic interest rates drastically. If the latter, we incur the risk of seeing our economic position undermined from fear of devaluation and still have no certainty that the rise in rates may not alarm foreigners overseas about the outlook for sterling more strongly than attracting them through the higher income offering on the money they have to lend.

It must be stressed that all this arises only on the count of external liquidity. We could get our exports and imports into better shape with rising productivity; we could slash our military commitments so that our balance of payments was running a surplus; we could even have a position in which our long-term lending abroad was balanced by long-term money coming into the United Kingdom; we could be satisfied that our price level compared more than favourably with other countries. Make all these favourable assumptions, and yet, through circumstances over which we have no control, there might come a rise in interest rates somewhere else in the world and we should be faced with a choice, either to raise our own rates (and so under-

[1] Later information appears to suggest that this may be on the low side.

mine a satisfactory economic position) or to see a flood of short-term money leave the country.

It must be stressed again that this external liquidity problem —the problem of owing short and being owed long—can exist quite independently of the better-understood difficulties arising out of spending too much while earning too little. Perhaps one should again remember the warning image of the manufacturer who, too successful in selling his goods, expands too rapidly and finds himself with delightful profits on paper and not enough cash to pay his wages on the Friday. He too has his stop–go, and very expensive it can be. If you have not got enough liquid capital it is dangerous as a country to go into the international banking business. And if you are in it already you had best move very cautiously indeed.

The key to the problem of external liquidity is to be found in the arrangements governing exchange rates. One can envisage three types of such arrangements which in appropriate circumstances are workable:

(i) Fixed exchange rates coupled with very adequate reserves (or at least automatically available long-term credit facilities which do not have to be renegotiated at intervals), which insulate the economy in respect of short-term movements of capital (or 'hot money' as it came to be called in the 1930s when it first became conspicuous).

(ii) Fixed exchange rates coupled with a far-reaching and effective control of overseas payments (and very probably trade as well).

(iii) Floating exchange rates coupled with an effectively managed internal economic position (for if you are to float you must know that if you go down you will come up again and will not sink to the bottom).

All three sets of arrangements, it will be noted, have their special methods of insulation as a protection from the pressures of the outside world. In the first case, reserves are adequate to

deal with an emergency and to buy time should any fundamental changes in the economy be desirable. In the second case
the protection is provided by exchange control, a method possible in war-time or in small compact countries with simple
trade relationships and efficient administrations, but much less
practical with peace-time trading and practices, or with large
countries involved in trading all over the world.

In the third case, the insulation is provided by the capacity
to float: if there is undue pressure on a currency, the rate drops
and holders of balances hesitate to take the loss involved in withdrawing them; and in any case speculators are exposed to the
danger that if they sell a currency short, they have no guarantee
that with no ceiling the rate may not rise very sharply when the
time comes for them to settle the transaction. With a rate that
can move sharply in either direction, rushes become unlikely
and speculators can be squeezed. Floating does not imply
devaluation in the sense of a fixing of a new parity at a lower
level. But it does imply satisfactory underlying conditions in the
domestic economy concerned; without this floating would become a gradual decline.

Looked at in this way, some of the underlying difficulties
involved in exchange-rate policy become apparent.

In a world thinking in terms of fixed rates alone, inadequate
reserves involve the problem of devaluation to a lower fixed
rate. The temptation to make too great a reduction is always
present; the risk of doing too little and having to devalue a
second time is not to be taken lightly. But an excessive devaluation means problems for the domestic economy, and new difficulties for other countries. In any case the threat of devaluation,
and the struggle to avoid it, will have created disturbance on its
own account: the speculation which comes in the form of
investing in commodities and goods whose price seems likely to
rise if the expected change takes place, and the consequent
increased stocks and imports.

But this is only the smaller part of the speculation involved.
If a country with inadequate reserves is threatened with devalu-

ation, the fixed rate provides the currency speculators with a most attractive one-way option. If the devaluation does take place, they make a gigantic profit. If the devaluation does not take place, the only loss is that of the cost of undoing the transactions, since the speculator is protected against a squeeze, because he knows he can always get his money at the old fixed rate. There is an opportunity for a speculator in effect to place a bet at 5 to 1 when the underlying chances would only justify even money. Such are the perils of fixed rates with inadequate reserves and large-scale international dealings.

Fixed rates supported by effective exchange controls are another matter. A small country whose currency is of domestic importance only may be able to run exchange control by seeing that it gets paid for what it sells and does not pay for what it has not had. But this does not apply to large industrialised economies, and even less to a world currency such as sterling. At best exchange control can only be a supplement to other policies. Stricter control over international financial dealings and over capital movements to the sterling area could help; but in the last resort they will not be strict enough to prevent a crisis.

A floating rate is a different matter. It has to be distinguished from a devaluation: the rate may go down, but in due course it can go up again. It may go up, if speculators get squeezed, but it can come down thereafter. The movement of funds is kept within reasonable dimensions. After 1931, once the U.S. dollar was devalued in terms of gold, the pound settled down at an exchange rate on the dollar higher than the original rate.

In present conditions—if the sterling price level is not out of line with other countries, and a comparison of prices does not suggest that it is—the departure of sterling from the existing parity in terms of other currencies will again have within it the possibility of a rebound and a return. Provided that we are controlling the domestic position and overseas Government outlay, the speculator has to take account of the fact that if he lets himself run short of sterling, the rate can temporarily go above the old rate. At the least it inhibits speculation.

For practical purposes, in a situation such as that with which we might be faced, there are more modest possibilities open to us. Instead of a rate moving within the limits of $2.78 to $2.82, there is the possibility of widening the range to, say, $2.60 to $3. This would combine the practical advantages of a reasonable measure of devaluation with the opportunity for restoring the position, and for good measure will add something for currency speculators to be frightened about. At any rate it would reduce the scale of hot-money movements.

Where does this diagnosis lead?

First, it does *not* suggest, as things stand, taking any steps on our own initiative in respect of exchange-rate policy. It assumes that U.K. prices may not be out of line with those elsewhere. It accepts that it is possible to eliminate the deficit on current account.

Second, it arrives at the conclusion that even if our current-account problems were to be solved by our own policies and exertions, we may be no longer left with a choice. The international monetary system is under great strain and pressure, quite apart from anything that may happen to the United Kingdom. There are three possibilities:

(a) That by international agreement a plan will be worked out which will take care of the international liquidity problem. Several such plans have been prepared, competent and imaginative plans. To work they will have to take account of the problems of the dollar and the pound as international currencies, in addition to more general aspects. If they do so, and provide sufficient support to enable the difficulties arising from the existence of international balances to be dealt with, the current strains disappear. But we must not deceive ourselves into believing that British influence can be a major force in bringing about such a satisfactory solution which requires international agreement.

(b) That a plan will be worked out which will represent the

highest common level of international agreement but one which does not fully take care of the liquidity problem or fails to deal with international currencies. For the U.K. there is the particular danger of a plan which may do something for the problems of a number of other countries, but fails to deal with the liquidity problem as far as sterling is concerned.

(c) That nothing is agreed, and the international monetary situation degenerates until an important currency—whether sterling or another—is compelled to abandon its present parity, and probably leads a movement in the same direction.

This analysis is very relevant to what happens if the outcome is (b) or (c). It is an exercise in contigency planning and it takes the form of a plea that if we find it impossible to hold the existing parity, we should not immediately tie ourselves to a lower rate, but should float (either within much wider limits or without any announced limits at all) and leave ourselves with room for manœuvre.

6. *International Acceptance Business as against International Deposit Banking*

This analysis has so far been in terms of exchange rates and the balance of payments. It also has implications from the angle of financing world trade.

At any moment of time a large volume of goods is in movement (or in preparation for movement) between countries. Much relates to consumption goods which will be paid for in cash or on short credit. But an important part of the rest consists of expensive capital goods to be paid for over years: engineering products, aircraft and ships, steelworks, pipelines, fertiliser plants and other projects. They will command medium- or long-term credit, anything from over six months to five years,

and even in exceptional circumstances up to ten years. Much of
such business is with countries which cannot afford to pay cash
at the outset, but can very well afford to pay over a period of
time. These are countries which do not need aid, but which
would have to cut back on their purchases but for credit:
countries such as Spain, Mexico, Venezuela and the other more
stable and prosperous parts of Latin America, the U.S.S.R. and
other countries of the Eastern bloc, China, and countries in the
Middle East.

These sales represent good business. The purchasers can
afford to buy as long as they are allowed to install the equipment and let it help to pay its way before all the money is due;
but they would be unable to meet the purchase price from the
very beginning.

Medium- and long-term credit is therefore a necessity if this
business is to be done. However, as things are at present, the
giving of credit must be the responsibility of the exporting
country, and an exporting country may well be in balance of
payments difficulties itself. Nevertheless, the supplier has to
finance the transaction whether his financial position on international account is weak or strong.

This is the consequence of the current practice of international deposit banking. A country's monetary authorities
have drawing rights on their accounts with the central banks of
other countries or on international institutions; they draw on
these balances to meet their outgoings; from time to time there
may be negotiations about the size of the advances which
may be made to reinforce these balances, and the terms on
which this is to be done if credit is to be given for this international business. These balances suffer when they are not replenished once the export takes place, but only after a lapse of
time.

The volume of funds tied up in respect of exports not yet paid
for is very substantial. To illustrate: Board of Trade figures
suggest that at the end of 1965 the U.K. was owed £1,300
million for such exports. Half of that was in respect of

short-term business, and some of the rest business between international companies and their overseas associates. But in these
figures there is a solid portion of medium- and long-term credit
of the type discussed—perhaps something of the order of £400
million. This refers to the U.K. alone. If we look at the total of
such outstanding medium- and long-term obligations arising
out of international trade in the world at any one time, it might
be of the order of $5,000 million or more. The exact figure is
immaterial; it is enough to establish that it is sufficiently large to
command attention.

This $5,000 million is in effect subscribed by the exporting
countries of the world to an international loan pool to finance
goods going on medium- and long-term credit from one country
to another. The debts owed to the exporting countries arise from
self-liquidating obligations, but are not liquid (i.e. immediately
realisable) assets. It is possible for them to be made realisable,
and so help those exporting countries—not only the U.K.—
which are in need of international liquid assets. What could
happen is that the exporter receives immediate cash, that the
buyer receives appropriate credit, and that the transaction is
financed by those countries which had surpluses on their
balance of payments and consequent foreign exchange at their
disposal which they could invest at interest. In short, the
proposal is that the link between exporting and financing
should be broken: the international loan pool of $5,000
million (or whatever it is) should be fed by those countries in
surplus so long as they remain in surplus; the exporter gets paid
cash and does not have the problem of providing credit at
the moment when he is in difficulties over his balance of payments.

There is technically no inherent difficulty in such an arrangement. To illustrate what is involved:

An exporter in country A undertakes to sell (say, a steel
mill) to country B. B undertakes to pay A over five years in
A's currency. When the project is technically completed, A
has promissory notes from B which he sells (through an

international market) to country C, and receives C's currency for the present value of the notes. A therefore has cash; C has the notes promising payment in A's currency. C will require assurance that he will be covered in respect of two eventualities: first, that of B defaulting; and second, that of A's currency (in which the contract is denominated) losing value in terms of C's currency before payment is made. These assurances A can readily give, and accept the obligations accordingly. This is because in the first place the price of the contract will have included an element of insurance against default and C will be the rightful beneficiary of this, since A will have received the premium. On the second point, A will have received payment in C's currency so that he can fairly accept the responsibility of repaying in C's currency. Assuming A has held C's currency, he will even have made a corresponding profit on the change of rate. The burdens are fairly distributed.

There is therefore no inherent objection to operating the international market on the basis of acceptances relating to specific self-liquidating international transactions, and the volume of finance which could be made available in this way might be quite considerable. What are the practical difficulties?

If one accepts the view set out above that it is only reasonable that the exporter who receives cash from the third country should both pass on the benefit of the credit insurance and undertake to guarantee repayment in the currency of the third country, that deals with one half of the question. The other half is more intractable. Can we in fact envisage the monetary authorities and banks of countries in credit on their international account making available funds for the purpose of acquiring obligations in respect of transactions to which they are not a direct party? The answer can be yes, but only if one assumes that they have excess reserves at their disposal which they have some inducement to lend at interest internationally. Under present conditions, in view of the general uncertainty, countries hesitate to admit that they have surpluses on their balance of payments, and even if they have, they hesitate even more to concede that these surpluses are in excess of their needs and available for tying up in this way. They tend to prefer to hold their reserves if possible in gold, or in foreign balances in an easily realisable form. In a different situation—for example, the conditions which would arise if there were a general devaluation as against gold of the type contemplated by the French—there might be excess reserves which monetary authorities could be anxious to invest, and even now monetary authorities do put money out in the Euro-dollar market. Although the prospects of an early development on the lines suggested may now appear remote, this need not always be so, and even as things are there could be room for some development in that direction.

Two consequential advantages emerge. For one thing, this method by which existing assets are mobilised to support actual self-liquidating transactions does provide an answer to charges of excessive credit creation, and avoids arguments about whether reserve quotas or drawings should be extended in order to cover extra business. The finance is only called for when specific transactions are undertaken, and to this extent controversy concerning the excessive credit might be removed from discussion.

The second advantage could in certain circumstances be far more important. This method enables financing to take place on the basis of the currency of the creditor, whoever he may be, and therefore does not depend on stable rates of exchange. It is a method which faces and deals with the problem of exchange-rate changes. If there were a reversion to fluctuating rates, such an approach might prove invaluable in maintaining world trade. Unlike international deposit banking, international acceptance business can be handled flexibly.

It might be added that such a device, quite apart from its usefulness as an expedient in an emergency, is not difficult to operate. It does not require any institution. It only needs a market, and an informal one at that. By operating in terms of the marketable currencies of all creditor countries (and not just in pounds and dollars), and doing so in respect of self-liquidating transactions, it could add stability to a world which large deposits of Euro-dollars may have unsettled.

THE EXTERNAL POSITION OF STERLING

in pounds and dollars, but due to in respect of difficulties the future owes. It could and stability to a world where large amounts of liabilities may have provided.

CHAPTER SEVEN

Financial Reform

1. *The Economic Deadlock*

We are faced in Britain with rising prices and wages in an economy where resources are fully employed; with the failure of productivity to increase in the way we might reasonably expect given technical progress and what others can do; with the persistent weakness of sterling and the balance of payments.

Nor can the difficulties be overcome by a simple direct attack. If we go hard for a policy of increasing productivity by increasing investment (with the ultimate aim of a greater output to keep prices lower and to provide more exports), the immediate effect of increasing investment would be to increase prices and displace exports. If, as an alternative, we attack rising prices by a policy of strict deflation in order to reduce demand and in the process increase exports, we hold back productivity and growth, and induce stagnation. Again, if we concentrate on large-scale measures to push output into exports, we are diverting supplies from the home market and increasing prices.

Simple solutions are not an answer. The easiest of them, that of a determined policy of deflation, is discredited by past experience. Between the wars prices were kept down, but at a terrible price in unemployment, and in the process we failed (in spite of fairly low interest rates) to get investment and modernisation which was much needed. Nor was there any spectacular increase in exports. The more modest stop–go interludes of recent years have had a restraining influence, but against this they also damaged productivity. The freeze-squeeze of July 1966 was a determined attempt to arrest the rise in prices, but its price was a reduction in the rate of growth.

A more complex approach is required. We are short both of industrial capacity and of labour. One cannot increase the supply of labour, leaving aside changes in social policy, and immigration in particular. But one can increase capacity through investment. Accordingly what we need is labour-saving investment: not the duplication of existing investment calling for a labour force that is not there, but new investment at the disposal of an existing labour force enabling an increase in output to be achieved.

This means that if we are to break the deadlock, we have to use an approach which on the face of it is contradictory. We must at one and the same time seek to restrain consumption while stimulating investment. Indeed it will be necessary to take the process of differentiation further and to select between the different types of investment chosen for stimulus.

Such an approach has to some extent been attempted for some time. It was reflected in investment allowances and initial allowances, which perhaps did not have all the effect that the ideas deserved. It now tends to take the form of cash payments to encourage investment. It could be reinforced by a tax system which since the Budget of 1965 leaves room, through the corporation tax, for lowering the rate on undistributed profits while raising income tax payable on profits distributed. It is at least theoretically possible to make the tax changes in opposite directions, and so bring a double pressure for the diversion of demand away from consumption towards investment.

How far can the monetary system act in a discriminatory manner so as to favour labour-saving investment while holding back other types of expenditure? Such an approach is not easy to manage. Investment is most profitable (and therefore most attractive) when demand is increasing. To stimulate investment when demand is being held back is a much more difficult operation. On the one hand a restriction in general consumption lowers the inducement to invest; on the other, a marked increase in investment could stimulate consumption and the consequent rise in prices and wages. The path is a narrow one which has to be followed carefully.

Nor are these the only difficulties that have to be surmounted. If one were to adopt a policy of increased taxes on consumption plus cheap finance for investment—which ultimately is the sort of thing which would have to be done if investment were to be safely stimulated—one must be prepared for unfavourable reactions in the balance of payments. A cut in interest rates could mean withdrawals of foreign money invested in London. The repercussions on the balance of payments would also need handling with care.

It is against a background such as this that one has to look at the financial machine. It is not just a question of its general efficiency but also one of seeing how far it is able to adapt itself to dealing with these delicate problems which arise when objectives have to be carefully selected with forces pulling in opposite directions. Problems of management will show themselves in three fields: in that of short-term finance and monetary control; in long-term capital supply in a world where prices are tending to rise; and lastly in the field of international payments, where the repercussions are not only on current account but also—given sterling's position as a world currency—on capital account as well.

2. *The Structure of Short-Term Finance*

An assessment of the mechanics of short-term finance must concern itself with somewhat intricate technical matters which can have far-reaching consequences. First, the nature of the arrangement by which very important business between the banks and the Bank is transacted through an intermediary, the discount market; is this an effective way of doing things now? Second, there is a considerable spread between rates charged on some kinds of business where the attendant risks and benefits would appear to be not dissimilar: local authority borrowing and Government borrowing are a case in point; how far is such a differentiation necessary or defensible? And where does it lead? Third, there are fields—the above is one example—where money from private sources is being tapped direct for purposes which in effect are in the public interest (i.e. the justification is the benefit which accrues to the community at large, rather than any income generated by the expenditure in question); what is the balance of advantage in such a treatment, and where is the line to be drawn between this and recognised public expenditure? Fourth, short-term money rates—following on movements in bank rate—seem to be much more volatile in the United Kingdom than in other developed countries; what are the consequences of this, and how far can they be mitigated, if necessary?

In looking at these questions, we are concerned not with general policy issues as such, but with the effectiveness of the machinery for handling the range of policies which may be called for in different situations as they arise.

The first concern was with the usefulness of the discount market as an intermediary between the banks and the Bank. The situation as it is now has developed over many years. In origin, this was a market in commercial bills, and it was only with war expenditure that it evolved into one mainly concerned with Government obligations—Treasury bills and bonds within sight of maturity. To the criticism that it seems surprising that twelve privately-owned houses should be undertaking at a profit work which could be done more simply and economically through an effective direct relationship between the banks and the Bank, the answer given is that the discount market has been rationalised to a considerable extent and is economical in its working,[1] and that even if the clearing banks worked more

[1] The Radcliffe Committee noted that the organisation of the discount houses is extremely simple: the total number of employees has been estimated at some 400. 'They are doing the work effectively, and they are doing it at a trifling cost in terms of labour and other real resources': Cmd. 827, 1959, paras. 163, 180.

directly with the Bank of England, a market in short-term obligations would still be needed for non-bank customers. The relationship between the Bank and the market, by which the market agrees to cover the Treasury bill tender and the Bank takes responsibility for ensuring that it is in a position to do so, is more difficult to explain; and it looks even more peculiar when as sometimes happens the Bank and the market do not see eye to eye about where the rate should be, and the market is forced to go to the Bank for assistance at penal rates. However, it can be argued in favour of the arrangement that the relationship between the banks and the Bank is made easier if it operates through a third party: this relationship is formalised with rules and conventions, and the strains of a confrontation between banks and Bank are thereby reduced. Nevertheless, the argument for or against a discount market of the type as we know it is not to be decided on these narrower grounds; what has to be settled is whether some other arrangement could give greater advantages.

This leads to the second question, which relates to the disparities in rates where risks and benefits are otherwise not dissimilar. The case of local authority finance in comparison with Government borrowing is by far the most important example. To illustrate again from figures published by the Bank of England:

	Treasury Bills	Local Authority Deposits	Difference
	(per cent per annum)		
End Dec. 1964	6·50	7·63	1·13
End June 1965	5·47	6·44	0·97
End Dec. 1965	5·44	6·38	0·94
End June 1966	5·66	6·38	0·72
End Dec. 1966	6·44	7·28	0·84

(The local authority deposit rates relate to rates for three months and thereafter seven days' notice.)

The difference between the two rates, although down, is not

to be accounted for by underlying disparities, even though Treasury bills are no doubt somewhat more convenient. On the one hand the lenders are protected: no one seriously expects that local authorities will be allowed to default. On the other, in neither case is the borrower protected against recall of the money; at the end of three months he has to be prepared to pay and reborrow. The difference is for the greater part unjustified, and must be accounted a defect in the financial machine. The fact that the higher rates may help to attract money from abroad is not a defence; it is not a function of local authorities to support foreign exchange. And the defect is a substantial one, with the outstanding short-term debt of the local authorities at over £1,800 million, three-quarters of it repayable on seven days' notice or less. A financing problem of this size is not conducive to financial stability.

This particular illustration leads to the general principle raised in the third question. This can be restated as follows. If one takes the view that a piece of financing is expedient in the community's interest (as opposed to a piece of business undertaken in the expectation of a profit), what is the case for its being financed by haphazard borrowing by subsidiary organs of Government? In a given economic situation a piece of expenditure by a public body must be settled on its merits. Once that question is decided—and it cannot just be left to the market if profitability is not relevant as a criterion—what remains is to see how it can most suitably be financed. The alternatives are either that local authorities should borrow in competition with each other on expensive terms which leave them precariously exposed with a vast quantity of short-term debt, or that the Government itself should raise the money—no doubt somewhat more cheaply, but quite possibly on short term on an inconveniently large scale—and relend it on more suitable terms through the Public Works Loan Board or otherwise to the local authorities. Admittedly the Government itself will then be faced with any problems arising from the existence of this volume of short-term debt, for which it will be responsible, but it is inconceivable that it could solve these difficulties by turning aside and leaving the local authorities to manage on their own. The outlay and the consequent demand on the real resources of the economy will be the same. To argue that in such circumstances it is better for the local authorities to borrow on fixed interest direct rather than for the Government to borrow on fixed interest on their behalf is not an acceptable proposition.

The position taken here amounts to saying that if the Government is satisfied that a piece of expenditure is necessary and that the material resources for it can be made available, it must be put in a position to carry through the relevant financing. If it is argued that the financial machine may be able to handle it as long as the borrowing is not made by the Central Government, but that there will be unfavourable repercussions if the Central Government does the borrowing itself, one can only conclude that in that case the machine is due for overhaul.

Before exploring what kind of changes may be needed if the Government is to handle an increased volume of direct borrowing, one must turn to the fourth of the questions set out earlier. It relates to the instability of money rates in the United Kingdom as compared with elsewhere.

This is not a matter of the general level of interest rates as such. As long as prices are continuing to rise, one must be prepared to see interest rates at a high level. The question is that of variations in interest rates over shorter periods of time. Once the business community has come to accept a given level of rates, it can make its plans accordingly. But if it is in a state of uncertainty as to whether rates are shortly going to move up or down, this is bound to affect decisions. Continuous planning is interrupted. The steady development of the domestic economy is prejudiced.

The instability of money rates in this country, as compared with others, arises from its exposed position on international account. Such movements of bank rate as might be necessary to maintain control of the domestic economy would have needed to be less frequent and smaller in scale than those we have

experienced. The big changes have come about because of outside pressure on the pound. Unfortunately, large movements in
bank rate carry with them correspondingly large movements
in the rates that industry has to pay for its advances; because
of this movements dictated by external pressures have had unhappy repercussions on the domestic economy.

Such a position is not a new one. Between the wars, the
Exchange Equalisation Account was intended to act as a buffer,
and to insulate the economy from the effects of movements of
hot money. More recent 'convertibility' coupled with inadequate resources to maintain this insulation has left us exposed to
the consequences of large-scale movements of short-term funds,
and the expedients and improvisations to which they have given
rise.

The possibility of restoring this insulation is taken up later.
The question of short-term finance in the domestic market
remains. And this domestic market has, as we have seen,[1]
developed into a number of markets—finance houses, local
authorities, Euro-dollars, inter-bank—all of which are evidence
of the large volume of the unfunded borrowings. The volume of
short-term borrowing by the local authorities speaks for itself,
and it is only one example. As long as unfunded liabilities exist
on such a scale, there must be danger of dislocation. Such
borrowing is sensitive to the flow of funds coming into the
market, and instability of rates results. The presence, directly or
indirectly, of foreign-owned balances in these markets adds to
the instability. We seem to be moving into an unreal world
where, the more finance-house and local authority borrowing
were to be reduced under the influence of a credit squeeze, the
resulting fall in interest rates could lead to the withdrawal of
foreign funds; successful austerity would thus bring with it the
reward of a flight from the pound because of the structure of the
market. Conversely, increased expenditure by the consuming
public or by local authorities could relieve our international
position because the rise in interest rates attracted foreign money

[1] Above, p. 83.

into the new markets. One must hope that this fantasy is exaggerated, that it is not as bad as all that. But to allow volatile foreign money to be built into an uncontrolled and ill-conceived structure of short-term obligations could expose us to severe penalties. The case for putting the temporary borrowing of the local authorities on a more permanent basis and for in-sulating and controlling the inflow of foreign balances (whether as Euro-dollars or otherwise) is that unless we do this, we can never be sure of being in control of our economic situation, however much we get our current balance of payments straight, or succeed in raising the rate of growth of our National Income.

As regards domestic financing, this means moving in the direction of the Government (i) taking over responsibility for a large part of the existing temporary borrowings of the local authorities, and (ii) becoming the source of finance for the greater part of the future net borrowings of the local authorities. While the amounts are large, it must be remembered that they have either been borrowed already or will have to be borrowed in any case in the future. The difference between borrowing by Government and by local authorities is technical. In the former case, borrowing on short term has importance for liquidity ratio and bank reserve purposes, and so can be the basis of further expansion. In the latter case it does not. Once the Government takes over this financial responsibility, it must therefore mean a substantial recasting of the banking and financial structure. It is not practical to attempt so large a task on the basis of the system as it is now.

To illustrate what is involved, one might assume (a) that £1,000 million of temporary borrowings are to be replaced (by degrees as opportunity offers) by a corresponding amount of loans from the Public Works Loan Board or some similar authority; and (b) that something of the order of £200 million per annum has to be found each year for capital expenditure which otherwise would have been financed by public bodies other than the Exchequer.

Certain consequences follow. To begin with, advances from

public funds will need to be made to pay off the temporary borrowings of the local authorities on the scale required. These loans will be repayable by the authorities over a period of years. But the money disbursed will show itself immediately in the cash of the clearing banks with the Bank of England. If it remains there, the 'cash' element is increased and can form the basis of further credit expansion; if, in one way or another, it is left in the form of Treasury bills with the banking system, the same result follows. There must therefore be deliberate countervailing action to sterilise any excessive element in this influx of cash. A call for added special deposits would be the conventional way of doing so at the moment.

Operations on this scale could, however, be carried through satisfactorily only if there were a much closer relationship between the Bank and the clearing banks. If money is to be found for local authorities, for financing exports or for industrial developments of special public interest, and if this is to be done without touching off an undesirable expansion of credit because of the added liquidity, the closest direct collaboration between the banks and the Bank is unavoidable.

In fact collaboration is already growing, and must go much further. Rather than lending call money to a discount market, it is logical that the clearing banks should hold excess balances with the Bank and receive interest on them. An appropriate proportion of these would be a part of the banks' liquid assets for ratio purposes. The conditions under which the remainder could be drawn on—or the interest withheld in the event of their premature use—would be part of the controlling mechanism for preventing an excessively liquid position developing. Indeed, one would envisage a situation in which a clearing bank has at the Bank of England not only its working account, and also, as at present, special deposits which are excluded from liquid assets, but other deposit (time) accounts on specified conditions representing other portions of the bank's assets with the Bank. A further possibility is that the bank, in its arrangements with the Bank of England, might have the equivalent of an 'overdraft limit' against which it could borrow in the event of need against assets of a certain prescribed character. Agreement about fixing and varying overall liquidity ratios, and instructions by means of 'requests' in respect of particular sectors of borrowing, would be a part of the enlarged machinery.

Arrangements of the kind set out could take many forms. The essential principle is that when large sums have to be disbursed from further funds for national purposes, care must be taken by collaboration between the central and commercial banks to ensure that the raising of the money does not give an undesirable impetus to expansion.

It follows that there will have to be corresponding changes in respect of the financial machinery outside the banks. An active direct relationship between the Bank and the banks leaves no room for the existence of a discount market in its present form. The indirect relationship by which the banks purchase their Treasury bills through the discount market instead of direct is cumbersome and gives rise to the odd situation in which the tender is always covered by special arrangement. While there may be room for a market in short-term obligations, Government and private, it should be a genuine private-sector market outside of the dealings between the Bank, the clearing banks and the Government itself.

The position of the banks other than the clearing banks presents a separate set of problems. If we take as an assumption that the Government has paid off something of the order of £1,000 million, we have as a first approximation: £1,000 million of reserves added at the Bank of England to the balances of the clearing banks, and a corresponding amount in favour of the non-clearing banks (and other intermediaries) added to their balance with the clearing banks. The balances with the Bank of England are—we have assumed—controlled: their use is circumscribed in such a way that they do not form the basis of undesirable additional lending. But there is no such restriction on the use to which the non-clearing banks and intermediaries put their balances.

The instantaneous picture of £1,000 million at both levels is of course artificial. From the beginning much of it will be invested in Government securities of one sort or another; the cash credited by Government will have been re-lent to the Government. Nor would the operation happen all at one go. But it is still necessary to provide for that element of the funds remaining with the non-clearing banks which could be used for lending purposes in circumstances which made this undesirable.

The problem exists already, and so far has been approached by the authorities on the basis of requests extended to these non-clearing banks not to increase the level of their lending above what it was in some previous period, or to observe the same criteria in respect of requests for loans as are being applied by the clearing banks. Powers—which might have to be conferred by legislation—would be needed to control these houses. Possibly they could provide for the equivalent of special deposits, either in the form of special non-transferable paper which would have to be taken up by each of the houses concerned in appropriate amounts, or alternatively through compulsory deposits at the Bank of England. It might even be necessary to prescribe limits on the scale of lending undertaken.

The lines of approach put forward here in respect of the machinery of short-term finance are thus threefold. In the first place, the position has got out of hand because of the existence of this great volume of short-term indebtedness on the part of the authorities, and because of the unavoidable requirements of the public sector taken as a whole. It is unfortunate that the local authorities are left to manage on their own. The Exchequer will have to take over. Second, to avoid undue liquidity being created in the banking system, a new relationship will have to be worked out between the Bank and the banks by which the latter carry a much higher proportion of their assets with the Bank on terms which prescribe their availability as a foundation of bank lending. Third, this control will have to be carried a stage further, so that the non-clearing banks in their turn are brought under control as regards their lending, and can be called on to provide special deposits or their equivalent.

The lines of development suggested for the short-term market are only a beginning. Two further aspects remain. On the one hand there is the question of the provision of long-term capital for Government and for business under conditions of rising prices. On the other, there is that of the foreign balances invested in London and liable to sudden withdrawal.

3. The Provision of Longer-Term Capital

British banks are basically short-term lenders. They are not willing providers of long-term capital. Their aim is to hold the accounts of borrowers who need finance for a continuing stream of business; as one piece of business is paid off, others take its place. The banks expect their advances to turn over.

As short-term lenders on fixed-interest terms, they are able to take a detached attitude towards their customers. As long as these are sufficiently prosperous, they can watch the money go out and come in. They do not participate directly in the fortunes of a business. If a business does well, they do not look for any share of the increased profits; if it does badly, they still expect to be paid without making concessions; and if its fortunes are in doubt, they will want a preferred position as against other creditors. Only in the case of disaster will they reluctantly be forced into taking any responsibility for the running of a business, and even then their wish will be to dispose of their involvement as soon as they can. Apart from taking a hand in hire-purchase finance houses over recent years, this traditional position has been maintained rigidly.

The converse of this is that business can look to the banks for finance only within limits. Productive industry in particular needs permanent capital over and above the working capital which the banks supply. A successful undertaking in course of expansion will find that the finance needed to sustain it is leading to increased indebtedness to the bank. The stage will then come when the process of growth makes it necessary for the business to raise more permanent capital to pay off the bank. At this point those in charge of the undertaking have to look beyond the banking system.

This is a natural development. As expansion takes place and more capital is required, bank advances are funded as equity shares or fixed-interest obligations are placed with investors. The speed and scale on which this can be done will depend ultimately on the absorptive capacity of the final purchasers of investments who are in a position to surrender liquid balances in return for more remunerative permanent holdings. If the process is working satisfactorily, as bank loans are paid off the banks have more money to lend. In some conditions of boom, the process may be working too fast, and restrictions may have to be put on bank lending to prevent it going too far either generally or in respect of particular forms of activity. In other circumstances the reverse may occur. Then the process may be going too slowly: the banks may be left with outstanding borrowings which are not being transformed fast enough into securities taken up by the investing public.

In this case the system is failing to work smoothly and is allowing congestion to occur. This may happen for two reasons. In the first place, there is sharp distinction between the two sets of institutions concerned. The banking system does not expect to have to make arrangements for the provision of permanent capital; the institutions of the capital market do not undertake large-scale temporary financing of industry. A second division is to be found in changes in the character of the obligations: private industry will in a large measure have to look to paying off debts through the issue of participating capital, dependent on its earnings. Either the circumstances of the company or conditions of the Stock Exchange may make the raising of new equity capital difficult.

Dependence on the Stock Exchange may become greater in a period of rising prices since it may be more difficult to borrow on fixed interest. Where industry has both to change sources of finance and to adjust its methods of raising capital in face of changes in the real value of money obligations, the technical problems become doubly complicated.

The break between the ordinary commercial banking system and the capital market is complete. The banks do not subscribe to or hold new issues, and they do not take the initiative in organising them. There are certain specialist finance houses which provide facilities for the smaller business. For the rest, where—as in most large cases—finance is to be obtained by marketing securities on the Stock Exchange, the services of an issuing house are required.

This relationship between finance and industry means that there is no common oversight of the financing problems of the more important industries such as an effective industrial banking system could give. A U.K. commercial bank is concerned with providing short-term money to credit-worthy borrowers. An issuing house is concerned to find businesses in search of capital who want to float issues on the Stock Exchange. Even in the case of a leading issuing house—such as one of the powerful merchant banks—the main responsibility is for giving advice on timing and methods of finance, and supporting the issue at critical moments until a wide distribution of the securities has been achieved with the investing public. Some large investors such as insurance companies may take a more continuous interest in what is happening, but in general there is no range of institutions whose business it is to look at the financing problems of an industry as a whole.

The test is that of whether any financial institutions have a continuing interest in the profits of a large group of companies, and use their control to promote orderly development and to stimulate expansion and investment. The answer as regards domestic industry in the United Kingdom is that such institutions are unimportant or non-existent. It is otherwise elsewhere: there is a much closer relationship between industry and finance in Western Europe, in the United States or in Japan, and even in the United Kingdom development overseas—gold-mining is a good example and very far from being the only one —has been organised by companies which start out with the object of finding finance and maintaining the necessary flow.

It could be argued that the inherent incapacity of the U.K. financial system to provide development finance has been responsible for the unhappy story of a number of innovations originating in the United Kingdom which have been brought to fruition elsewhere. This country was among the first to have motor-scooters; they were developed in Italy. We were the first with television, but the 625-line system now in use was introduced from abroad, while in the discussion of colour television the merits of systems from the Continent and North America are being canvassed, without any British contender. Aircraft with variable wings were invented in this country, but developed in the United States. Once we were in the forefront of those developing computers, but are now behind in the scale on which they have been introduced. Examples of this sort may not be conclusive, but there is a case to answer. The story could hardly have been quite the same if there existed strong supporting finance pressing for the exploitation of new outlets. Commercial banks trying to restrict themselves to short-term lending and issuing houses whose purpose is to distribute securities cannot be assumed to be enough.

These difficulties are made more acute by a new factor which has arisen in the post-war period: the steady increase in prices in a world of full employment. This may not go above the rate of 3½ per cent which we have been experiencing over past years, and it is fervently to be hoped that it will be less. But it is difficult to believe that we can avoid some continuing increase, though possibly on a modest scale.

The implications of rising prices are far-reaching for the shape which financial obligations are likely to take. The arithmetic speaks for itself. If someone is to take up a long-term fixed-interest loan when prices rise at an annual rate of 3½ per cent, this means that before he gets any return at all he must receive

3½ per cent net of any tax. To get a net return of 2 per cent and maintain the real value of the loan therefore calls—assuming the prospective investor is an average taxpayer—for nominal rates of interest in the range of 8–10 per cent. Even if the rate of price increases is brought well below 3½ per cent, the nominal rates must still look high compared with those current during periods of price stability. As a practical matter, one is driven to the conclusion that on any assumption the volume of long-term fixed-interest lending which the market will be able to absorb must be limited. It will certainly be much less than the demand, because rising prices mean for the borrower a decreasing real burden of debt. Governments naturally borrow on fixed interest. Private borrowers have every inducement to do the same, if they can get the money. As the real burden of prior charges lightens, the benefit of higher prices adds to the value of the equity.

In this situation, what form will the provision of long-term capital finance tend to take?

First, one must look to a much higher proportion of equity finance wherever such finance is appropriate, because with rising prices and a diminishing real burden of debt the enterprise can offer better prospects for its proprietors. One must expect a large increase in equity financing as the scope for long-term fixed-interest borrowing is reduced.

Second, one must expect a greater volume of hybrid obligations taking the form of convertible loan stock, or something similar. A given rate of interest is offered in the first instance as a prior charge, but the holder is given rights—under defined conditions—to convert into ordinary shares or the equivalent, and this right becomes valuable if the company prospers. This can be made an attractive inducement, and one must expect the volume of convertible loan stock to increase.

The third method is that of index bonds. The prearranged rate of interest in this case may be relatively low, but it will be linked to some index of purchasing power, so that the payments increase in money terms to the extent necessary to maintain the original purchasing power. Something of this sort is already inherent in arrangements by which leases are renegotiated at intervals and adjusted to current values. But index bonds are a very drastic step.

Lastly, there is the possibility of tax concessions to mitigate the effects of rising prices in the case, for example, of Government borrowings or of borrowings which the Government decides to facilitate in the public interest. This again involves an index of purchasing power. The concept could be that to the extent that prices rose, the interest would be free of tax. Thus assuming a 5 per cent obligation, and a price rise of 3 per cent during the year, tax would only be payable on the excess 2 per cent. It is not the purpose here to advocate a particular device; but when the gilt-edged market is crumbling this is a method which might serve to maintain Government fixed-interest borrowing without going so far as index bonds, with their drastic consequences.

What emerges is that as things have gone it is not enough to have a system of banks with their short-term lending, together with separate issuing houses handling the raising of money on the Stock Exchange. The importance of integrated financial arrangements, and the technical conditions of the capital market in face of rising prices, call for major changes in the organisation of the facilities for providing capital.

A solution is possible on the following lines. The clearing banks would accept that the restriction to short-term lending was no longer tenable as regards their business customers. They would have to be prepared to hold, where necessary, ordinary shares both in anticipation of their being issued to the public and to some extent also rather more permanently where particular companies had to be nursed or major industrial developments were due to be undertaken. They could, for administrative reasons, segregate these activities in their own special subsidiaries; there is no need directly to mix up advance business and the holding of shares. But these subsidiaries would be more than investment trusts. On the one hand they could not avoid having some responsibility for the active management of some of the companies, in particular those embarking on new developments. On the other hand, as developments matured, they would carry through all the functions at present carried out by issuing houses, up to the point where the securities were successfully floated through the Stock Exchange.

If the argument is accepted up to this point, the next stage follows. The banks should seek to absorb selected merchant banks (who combine the functions of banking, accepting, issuing and financial advisers) and incorporate them within their groups. This suggestion springs in part from the view that the future of the merchant banking houses is not assured when the public interest requires that active business of international account should be curtailed, and that something less haphazard should replace present methods of floating stocks and shares and conducting competitive takeover bids. But it is also recognised that these sources have much in the way of skill and technique which should be usefully harnessed. Such acquisitions will bring new blood to the commercial banks, and put them into a position to carry out the wider responsibilities contemplated. Some merchant banks would no doubt prefer to stay independent, though they would be faced with the direct competition of commercial banks in some fields that they had looked on as their own. But many others could benefit by the direct connection. On the one hand the banks would be going a long way into business; on the other, the expertise of the merchant banks would be allied to the financial resources of the banks, and both would be brought into more direct touch with the ramifications of domestic industry.[1]

Looking at what is proposed for the banking system as a whole, major changes are involved. This is a plea, at the short

[1] In December 1966 the National Provincial Bank and N. M. Rothschild and Sons announced the joint formation of a new banking subsidiary, but it would appear to be directed to attracting deposits in the international money markets rather than to providing capital for home industry.

end, for a more co-operative and direct relationship between the banks and the Bank, cutting out the discount market. At the long end, it is a plea for extending the scope of the banks in organising the supply of capital, by incorporating in them work done by merchant banks in their capacity as issuing houses and otherwise, and by adding further a responsibility for nursing and holding equity capital in the undertakings of their customers.

4. *Sterling and International Payments*

The external problems of sterling have already been discussed at length. What follows takes the form of notes on three particular issues: the interest-sensitive external balances; the prospects of a satisfactory agreement on the world liquidity problem; and the future price of gold.

First, the interest-sensitive balances. Reasons have been given for believing they are large. They have attained their size as a consequence of the policy of supporting the forward exchange. Such support was intended to avert an immediate threat of withdrawal at the price of a postponement, it was hoped until things became better. It must have seemed a reasonable price to pay for such a postponement.

However, the concession having been made, it became the basis of further short-term borrowing. Foreign balances were attracted to London once they enjoyed both higher interest rates and an exchange guarantee available at a price which still left a margin. A defensive measure, adopted to discourage withdrawals, developed into a method of external borrowing, profitable to those financial houses that came to handle the business. Consequently a large volume of such short-term market borrowings was superimposed on the borrowings arranged by the U.K. authorities from other central banks and the International Monetary Fund. However, these commercial borrowings are a first charge, in the sense that if interest rates fall (or indeed any threat to sterling becomes widespread) the money goes out. This is a fact which cannot be ignored.

Two conclusions emerge. On the one hand, any straightening-out of the short-term money markets will have to take account of the existence of these balances. If differential interest rates have to be maintained under any future reorganisation in order to ensure the presence of the money, this would seem better done by special arrangement through the machinery of the Exchange Equalisation Account and not in the open market. Both the volume and the recipients of the privilege of this higher rate will therefore be under supervision. This will require delicate handling because the pressure for the higher rate will be maintained. The houses dealing in the money could prefer to withdraw money which no longer gets the benefit of higher interest rates in this country, rather than recall money on-lent to American companies prepared to pay well for it. In so far as the banking houses are guided by considerations of profitability alone, it is the money swapped into sterling and lent in the U.K. that will be in the front line for withdrawal. However, experience in the United States has shown that much can be done by moral pressure, and in this country such pressure could be reinforced through the importance attached to recognition as an authorised dealer in foreign exchange.

The second conclusion follows from this. Quite apart from these temporary short-term borrowings, we owe money to other central banks and to the I.M.F. As we begin to earn something on our current balance of payments, or receive proceeds from the repatriation of realised overseas investments, we should use these proceeds to pay off any volatile balances before we pay off the official creditors. It may not be easy to make the central banks and other creditors appreciate this, but so long as these balances continue in London at the expense of high rates and exchange guarantees, we cannot be our own masters, and free to adopt a policy leading to increased production and the consequent strengthening of our balance of payments. These foreign balances must be a first charge on our earnings when we begin to pay our way if we are to be in the position of other countries which actively control the inflow of foreign money.

The second main issue was that of the prospects of a satisfactory international agreement on the world liquidity problem. Whatever one's views as to the prospects of this coming about, in theory it is possible to devise such an agreement. In practice, differences remain between those whose collaboration will be needed. As yet there is no sign that the differences will be resolved. But Britain's voice is no longer loud in these matters, and we shall have to guard against something being arranged which represented the maximum of agreement attainable but would nevertheless bind this country to an agreement which fell short of her needs and left us with obligations we could not appropriately fulfil without weakening the economy. It may not be easy to withstand pressure to accept something damaging on the ground that it is the best that our negotiators can do. But if we remain tied, it may be impossible to get the economy moving. Provided we curb our overseas expenditures and commitments, the current balance of payments should be manageable, and if pressure is brought on sterling, it would be better to let the rate slide temporarily, rather than dissipate dwindling resources in a losing attempt to hold it.

Lastly, the price of gold. This is at the centre of the main differences of opinion between the leading financial countries. The French, one understands, favour a substantial increase in the price of gold; this would be to their benefit in view of their large gold holdings. The Americans would appear to be opposed to any increase in the price of gold, and take the view that arrangements for the creation of credit on an international basis could deal with the world liquidity problem. The French position is logical, in the sense that once there were a substantial increase in the price of gold, the international credit position would be eased and it could subsequently be controlled with less dissension by closer reference to gold movements. The weakness of this approach is that there is no clear reason why the need for credit should follow the distribution of gold holdings at the moment when a readjustment of the price of gold took place.[1] In the meantime, the French are building up their gold holdings, and the Americans are seeking to persuade other countries to hold dollars rather than build up theirs.

Opinion in the world at large expects an increase in the price of gold; that is why gold hoarding is at so high a level. Only a small proportion of the new gold becoming available each year finds it way into monetary reserves. One possible condition is that if the price of gold does go up, gold coming out of hoards and swelling the monetary reserves of the developing countries will enable the latter to speed up development through increased purchases of capital goods from the industrial countries.

Against such a background of strain, Britain is left without much choice, and with the possibility that the choice will be made for her. In such circumstances, all this country can seriously contemplate is to control the domestic economy, curb external payments,[2] and if forced off her existing exchange parity, avoid fixing a new one. In short, a floating pound, the necessary measures to prevent it sinking, and a wait to see what happens elsewhere. There is no need to be stampeded into the view that sterling will permanently lose value against the general run of other currencies. This includes the dollar.

Further, we should remind ourselves that the fact that a number of currencies are floating need not be allowed to destroy the basis of payment for world trade. A closer linking between specific international transactions and the international provision of finance for them, of the kind discussed under the heading of international acceptance business,[3] shows that there

[1] There are possibilities of handling a revaluation in such a way as to distribute the resulting profits on a basis which could be defined as fair. See J. R. Cuthbertson, 'Gold Revaluation without Tears', *The Banker* (January 1963).

[2] This must mean large, urgent and genuine reductions, in particular of Government overseas military expenditure. To earmark hard-pressed productive capacity for arms, etc., for sale to foreign Governments to provide foreign exchange in order to maintain commitments abroad would not meet the case. All available capacity will be needed for our own purposes.

[3] Above, pp. 154–9.

are possibilities of working even a system of long-term credit under conditions of monetary fluctuation.

5. *Some Further Implications of Liquidity*

In conclusion it may be relevant to reflect on some of the implications of the line of approach which has been attempted in this book.

It will be recalled that from the outset this approach was developed on the basis of the concept of liquidity, coupled with an uncompromising rejection of hard-and-fast concepts of money as something quantitatively measurable. Liquidity derives from the balance of assets and liabilities, present and prospective, and is to be interpreted not in terms of the mere size of the difference between them, but in the capacity which they give to their possessor, after weighing both sides of the account, to enter into further obligations. Liquidity therefore turns on how far and when assets are easily realisable, and the timing of liabilities falling due for payment. Payment takes the form of cancelling obligations against claims. The machinery of cancellation is, for the most part (but not exclusively), operated through the banking system. Control of the means of payment therefore comes to mean control of access to the cancellation process, this access taking the form of having a balance at the bank, or being able to acquire one by selling an asset, or by being able to borrow from the bank. The concept of liquidity parts company with the concept of money because the liquidity of its possessors is not something that can be aggregated, while the concept of money which is discarded here assumes that money can.

This book—in intention—seeks to demonstrate that liquidity has a practical bearing on certain urgent matters. First, on the external position of sterling it is argued that—quite apart from any failure to make ends meet on current international account —there is an inherent and continuing weakness because we have been acquiring short-term balances which are liable to be withdrawn in circumstances over which we have no control; and this can happen at a time when the corresponding assets are not in a liquid (i.e. adequately realisable) form. Second, in considering the supply of long-term capital, the effect of rising prices was shown to be to undermine the position of fixed-interest borrowers, including in particular the public authorities, by forcing them to enter into obligations which they might have to meet at short notice, while putting lenders into a position where these quick assets could be realised quickly for the purpose of making payments at a time when additions to demand might be economically undesirable. Third, in examining the structure of the short-term money markets it was shown that the growth of short-term obligations had led to liquidity on a scale which made special measures of control necessary for domestic reasons, and further had brought with it a damaging dependence on foreign funds.

These are all practical matters. There are also some more general consequences of substance.

In the first place, it will be recalled that in place of a given amount of money (bank balances) and an independent velocity at which it circulated, it could be shown that money and velocity were interchangeable in the following circumstances. A bank both borrows money from some of its customers (at a lower rate) and lends to others (at a higher rate). If it is approached for a loan, which is given and disbursed, the deposits of the banking system are raised accordingly. But the transactions can be financed in another way. The borrower (if he thinks the bank is proposing to charge too much) has the option of seeking out someone who already has a balance with the bank and borrowing from him direct. In that case, the deposits of the banking system will not increase when the loan is disbursed; what has happened is that the existing deposits have revolved that fraction more rapidly. An understanding of this (and its converse) is essential if the problems of monetary control are to be seen clearly, and the liquidity approach, with its emphasis on capacity to enter into obligations, helps to bring out the issues involved.

Second, liquidity is a concept which helps to bring out the fact that a payment from A to B need not have equivalent effects on the giver and receiver. Although the sum of money that passes is one and the same, the extent to which A's liquidity is reduced need not be the same as the extent to which B's liquidity is increased; the latter may be greater or less. We need to know the structure of assets and liabilities of both of the parties involved before we can conclude that the capacity of the one to enter into new transactions is reduced to the same extent as that of the other is increased.

This has consequences which go deeper. In comparing alternative investment possibilities for a given output, current practice would, on the basis of comparable data, assess the present value of the projected outlay and income over time, using some Discounted Cash Flow or similar approach. But this does not settle the matter. The liquidity point is simply this: one method may involve a higher peak borrowing than the other, irrespective of comparative profitability. Therefore *for the same projected output* and faced with exactly the same technical alternatives, the poorer undertaking may have to adopt the less economical method for liquidity reasons alone.

The emphasis here is on 'for the same projected output'. This is nothing to do with economies of scale or with richer companies being able to do things bigger and better than poorer ones. It boils down to the proposition that the constriction of borrowing power in the case of a company faced with a given demand may force it to adopt a less economical method for meeting that demand. The method ruled out could be—indeed is likely to be? —one involving labour-saving investment. The argument will not be pursued further here, but could seem to run in the direction of underwriting labour-saving investment in the case of undertakings which otherwise could only afford investment involving a higher demand for labour.

Lastly, one general reflection may be added. The concept of

liquidity, with its starting-point of the evaluation of the position by each possessor of assets and liabilities, carries with it the implication that effective decision-making is becoming more widely diffused. The analysis put forward suggests that general credit policy administered on the basis of a limited number of decisions from above cannot give the necessary guidance to the economy. The need for control of lending policy at more levels and in greater detail arises not only from the immediate economic circumstances in which we are situated, but also from the way things are going. As we get richer in the goods we possess and in the value of the land and property we own, we grow in our capacity to use our wealth as the basis for extending the scope of the transactions into which we enter or the speculative positions we build up. The built-in protections are not what was once supposed. With the diffusion of wealth, we need a corresponding diffusion in techniques of control and in the exercise of responsibility.

Index

Accepting houses, 44 n., 92, 93
Agricultural Mortgage Corporation, 45
Assets and liabilities: of discount market, 78, 79; offset between, 16–18; overall extent of, in U.K., 20 n.; return on assets, 35, 36; scope and nature of, 25–9, 37, 38

Balance of payments (U.K.): causes of current weakness, 123–5, 147–8; components of, 121–3
Bank advances, 69, 72, 73, 100, 101
Bank deposits: competition for, 62–7, 99, 100; determination of volume of, 62–7; figures of, 61, 92, 93; reasons for holding, 61, 62
Bank for International Settlements, 133, 137, 138, 139, 140
Bank of England: and clearing banks, 68–73, 107, 169, 170; and discount market, 80–3, 170
Bank of England Quarterly Bulletin, 68, 98 n., 107, 133 n., 140, 148 n.
Bank rate, 49, 69, 70, 103, 104
Banks, clearing: analysis of assets, 68–73; and competition from financial intermediaries, 62–7, 77, 99, 100; confined to short-term lending, 172; facilities of, 41, 42, 48, 50–2; suggested extension to equity financing, 177–9
Banks, overseas, 45, 92, 93, 148
Banks, Scottish and Northern Ireland, 90, 92
Building Societies, 48, 50, 91, 112
Business funds: employment of, 57–61

Capital: for enterprise, 105–7, 120, 172–9

Cash ratio (of clearing banks), 69, 98, 101–4
Convertible loan stock, 176
Cramp, A. B., 104 n.
Credit: creation of, 73–8, 184; importance of availability of, 111–13; limitations on, 69–72, 77, 78
Credit control: discriminatory, 107, 108, 119, 120; general quantitative, 97–107, 119; hire-purchase, 108; implications of, 114–20, 184; and money rates, 109–14; scope, 95–7
Crouch, R. L., 102 n.
Cuthbertson, J. R., 182 n.

Decision-making, greater diffusion of, 186
Discount market, 43, 44, 69, 70, 78–83, 163, 164, 179
Discounted Cash Flow, 185

Effective demand: and fiscal measures, 114–19; significance of, 12–14, 95–6
Einzig, Dr. Paul, 133 n., 136, 141
Euro-currencies (other than dollars), 133–4
Euro-dollars: borrowers of, 139; in conditions of strain, 143–5; defined, 131–133; and forward exchange rates, 141, 149; London dollar Certificates of Deposit, 142–3; London market in, 83, 132, 141; operations in, 141, 142; reasons for, 134–6; restrictions on, 141 n.; sources of, 136–7, 139; U.K. position, 140, 145–7; use of, 138; volume, 133
Exchange Equalisation Account, 127, 167, 180

Exchange rates (*see also* Sterling): and convertibility, 125, 126, 129–32; fixed, 125, 126, 129, 150–2; floating, 125, 127–9, 150–4, 182, 183; forward, 141, 149

Export credit, 70, 86, 108

Finance Corporation for Industry, 45

Finance for innovations, 174, 175

Financial intermediaries: Bank of England control over, 171; in competition with clearing banks, 62–7, 76, 77, 83, 84

Financial reform, possibilities of: in respect of longer-term capital, 172–9; short-term finance, 162–72; sterling's international position, 179–82

Financial system: outlined, 41–6

Foreign balances, 147–9, 167, 168, 179, 180, 184

Freeze/squeeze of July 1966, 55, 56, 160

Full employment, 13, 161

General Theory of Employment, Interest and Money, 12, 16

Gold, 131, 181, 182

Government debt: effect of balance of payments on, 85; and investment, 84, 85, 165, 166; possible increase in, 86–9, 165, 166; relation to market, 98–9

Grant, A. T. K., 37 n., 106 n., 125 n.

Hire-purchase finance houses, 48, 51, 83, 91, 140, 141

I.B.R.D. (International Bank for Reconstruction and Development), 130

I.M.F. (International Monetary Fund), 130, 179, 180

Index bonds, 176, 177

Industrial and Commercial Finance Corporation, 45

Insurance companies, 90

Inter-bank market, 83

Interest rates: concept of single rate, 15, 35; instability of short-term rates, 167; objectives of policy, 113–14, 120; structure of, 16, 35, 36, 109–13

International liquidity: Fund's attitude towards, 130, 131, 181; planning for, 153, 154, 181; position of reserve currencies, 130, 131

International trade: financed by third parties, 157, 158; and fluctuating exchanges, 158; funds tied up in financing, 155, 156; and self-liquidating finance, 157–9

Investment, domestic: financing in public sector, 165–6; problems and methods of stimulating, 160–2

Issuing houses, 44 n., 93

Kahn, Richard (Professor Lord Kahn), 115

Keynes, J. M. (Lord Keynes), 12, 115

Liquid assets ratio (of clearing banks), 69–72, 98, 102

Liquidity (*see also* International liquidity): external (of U.K.), 149, 150, 184; implications of, 37–40, 95, 96, 183, 184, 185; and indebtedness of public sector, 84–9, 184; and insolvency, 29–31; and money, 31–5; nature of, 17, 18; possible contradiction between liquidity and profitability, 185; and spending, 95, 96

Local authorities' borrowing, 83, 87, 140, 141, 163–5, 168, 169, 184

'London's "New" Markets for Money', 83

Merchant banks, 44, 92, 178, 179

Money: in the form of notes and coins, 22, 23; Quantity Theory of, 34; subsidiary role of, 18, 38, 39; traditional views of, 14, 15, 31–4

Money markets (*see also* Discount market), 83, 119, 167

'Multiplier', 115–18

National Development Bonds, 49–53

Newlyn, W. T., 102 n.

Obligations: under barter conditions, 21, 22; capacity for entering into, 39; settlement of, 22–5; structure of, 20–2

Payment: by cancellation through banking system, 17, 18, 23–5, 38; by means of coins and notes, 23, 31–2, 38; unequal effects on liquidity, 39, 185

Posner, M. V., 104 n.
Post Office Savings Bank, 49–53
Premium Savings Bonds, 49–51, 53
Public Works Loan Board, 165, 168

Radcliffe Committee, 37 n., 44 n.,
   163 n.
Revell, J., 20 n.
Rising prices: effect on fixed-interest
   lending, 53, 54, 175, 176; and possible
   tax concessions, 54, 177

Savings: effect of rising prices on, 53,
   54; effect of taxation on, 51–4; outlets
   for, 46–51
Savings Certificates, 49–53

Sayers, R. S., 37 n.
Short-term overseas debt (of U.K.),
   147–9
Special deposits, 69, 72, 82–3, 102
Sterling, external position: between
   1919 and 1939, 125–8; after 1945,
   128–32; in 1967, 147–9
Stock Exchange, 42, 44, 45, 54, 105,
   106, 174, 177

Treasury bills, 60, 69, 70, 80, 87, 98,
   163–5, 170
Trustee Savings Banks, 48, 50, 51, 53,
   90, 91

Unit trusts, 90